ENGLISH
FOR EVERYONE

LIBRO DE ESTUDIO

NIVEL 1 INICIAL

AUDIO GRATUITO
web y app
www.dkefe.com

Autora

Rachel Harding tiene una larga experiencia como profesora de inglés y actualmente se dedica de manera exclusiva a escribir materiales para la enseñanza de este idioma. Ha publicado en las principales editoriales de este campo, entre las cuales la Oxford University Press.

Consultor del curso

Tim Bowen ha enseñado inglés y ha formado profesores en más de 30 países en todo el mundo. Es coautor de libros sobre la enseñanza de la pronunciación y sobre la metodología de la enseñanza de idiomas, y autor de numerosos libros para profesores de inglés. Actualmente se dedica a la escritura de materiales, la edición y la traducción. Es miembro del Chartered Institute of Linguists.

Consultora lingüística

La profesora **Susan Barduhn** cuenta con una gran experiencia en la enseñanza del inglés y la formación de profesores. Como autora ha participado en numerosas publicaciones. Además de dirigir cursos de inglés en cuatro continentes, ha sido presidenta de la Asociación Internacional de Profesores de Inglés como Lengua Extranjera y asesora del British Council y del Departamento de Estado de Estados Unidos. Actualmente es profesora de la School for International Training en Vermont, Estados Unidos.

ENGLISH FOR EVERYONE

LIBRO DE ESTUDIO

NIVEL 1 INICIAL

Edición Gareth Clark, Lisa Gillespie, Andrew Kerr-Jarrett
Edición de arte Chrissy Barnard, Ray Bryant
Edición de arte sénior Sharon Spencer
Asistencia editorial Jessica Cawthra, Sarah Edwards
Ilustración Edwood Burn, Denise Joos, Michael Parkin,
Jemma Westing
Producción de audio Liz Hammond
Dirección editorial Daniel Mills
Dirección de la edición de arte Anna Hall
Dirección del proyecto Christine Stroyan
Diseño de cubierta Natalie Godwin
Edición de cubierta Claire Gell
Dirección de desarrollo del diseño de cubierta Sophia MTT
Producción, preproducción Luca Frassinetti
Producción Mary Slater
Dirección de la edición Andrew Macintyre
Dirección de arte Karen Self
Dirección general editorial Jonathan Metcalf

DK India
Diseño de cubierta Surabhi Wadhwa
Dirección editorial de cubierta Saloni Singh
Diseño sénior DTP Harish Aggarwal

De la edición en español
Coordinación editorial Elsa Vicente
Asistencia y producción Malwina Zagawa

Publicado originalmente en Gran Bretaña en 2016 por
Dorling Kindersley Limited DK, One Embassy Gardens, 8 Viaduct
Gardens, London, SW11 7BW. Parte de Penguin Random House

Título original:
English For Everyone. Course Book. Level 1. Beginner
Undécima reimpresión: 2024

Servicios editoriales: Tinta Simpàtica
Revisión pedagógica y traducción: Lola Thomson-Garay (Elastic)
Revisión de la traducción: Anna Nualart

ISBN: 978-1-4654-6216-9

Impreso y encuadernado en China

Todas las imágenes © Dorling Kindersley Limited
Para más información, ver www.dkimages.com

www.dkespañol.com

Contenidos

Cómo funciona el curso

English for Everyone está pensado para todas aquellas personas que quieren aprender inglés por su cuenta. Como cualquier curso de idiomas, cubre las habilidades básicas: gramática, vocabulario, pronunciación, escucha, conversación, lectura y escritura. A diferencia de otros cursos, todo ello se practica y aprende de forma enormemente visual, con el apoyo de gráficos e imágenes que te ayudarán a entender y a recordar. La mejor manera de progresar es seguir el libro por orden utilizando el audio de la web y la app del curso, y hacer las tareas del libro de ejercicios al acabar cada unidad para consolidar con la práctica lo aprendido.

LIBRO DE EJERCICIOS

LIBRO DE ESTUDIO

Número de unidad El libro está dividido en unidades. El número de unidad te ayuda a seguir tu progreso.

Qué vas a aprender La unidad comienza con un resumen de lo que aprenderás en ella.

Módulos Cada unidad se compone de distintos módulos que debes seguir por orden. Puedes tomarte un descanso tras completar cualquiera de ellos.

Aprendizaje del idioma Las secciones con fondo de color te presentan nuevo vocabulario y gramática. Estúdialas con atención antes de ponerte a hacer los ejercicios.

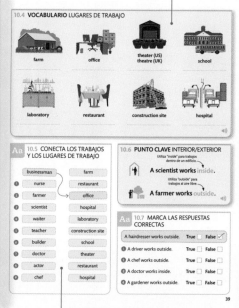

Audio de apoyo La mayoría de los módulos cuentan con audio grabado por hablantes nativos que te ayudará a mejorar tu expresión y tu comprensión.

Ejercicios En los módulos con fondo blanco tienes ejercicios para practicar lo aprendido y consolidar las nuevas habilidades.

AUDIO GRATUITO
web y app
www.dkefe.com

Módulos de idioma

Cada nuevo apartado se presenta gradualmente: comienza por una explicación básica de cuándo se aplica, da a continuación ejemplos reales de uso y termina con un análisis detallado de cómo funcionan las estructuras clave.

Número de módulo
Cada módulo tiene su propio número, para que puedas seguir tu progreso y te sea fácil localizar el audio correspondiente.

Titular del módulo
El tema que se va a tratar aparece aquí junto con una breve introducción.

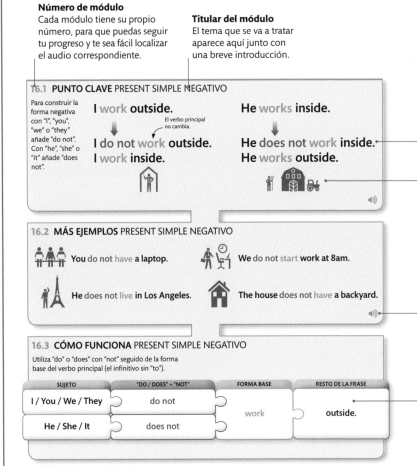

16.1 PUNTO CLAVE PRESENT SIMPLE NEGATIVO

Para construir la forma negativa con "I", "you", "we" o "they" añade "do not". Con "he", "she" o "it" añade "does not".

I work outside.
El verbo principal no cambia.
I do not work outside.
I work inside.

He works inside.
He does not work inside.
He works outside.

Frases de ejemplo Cada nuevo apartado se presenta en contexto. Los destacados en color y las notas explicativas facilitan la comprensión de las nuevas estructuras.

Guía gráfica Ilustraciones sencillas y claras ayudan a entender el sentido de las nuevas formas y a saber cuándo usarlas, y facilitan su aprendizaje y su recuerdo.

16.2 MÁS EJEMPLOS PRESENT SIMPLE NEGATIVO

You do not have a laptop.

We do not start work at 8am.

He does not live in Los Angeles.

The house does not have a backyard.

Audio de apoyo Este símbolo indica que las frases de ejemplo del módulo están disponibles en grabaciones de audio en la web y la app.

16.3 CÓMO FUNCIONA PRESENT SIMPLE NEGATIVO

Utiliza "do" o "does" con "not" seguido de la forma base del verbo principal (el infinitivo sin "to").

SUJETO	"DO / DOES" + "NOT"	FORMA BASE	RESTO DE LA FRASE
I / You / We / They	do not	work	outside.
He / She / It	does not		

Guía de formación Estas guías visuales desmenuzan la gramática inglesa en sus componentes básicos para mostrar gráficamente cómo funcionan incluso las estructuras más complejas.

Vocabulario A lo largo del libro tienes módulos de vocabulario que recogen las palabras y las expresiones más útiles del inglés, e incluyen pistas visuales que te ayudarán a recordarlas.

Espacio para escribir Es útil que escribas la traducción de los términos, pues tendrás así tus propias páginas de referencia.

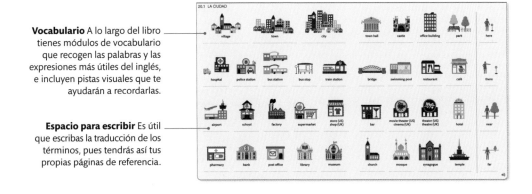

Módulos de ejercicios

Cada ejercicio está cuidadosamente graduado para que profundices y contrastes lo que has aprendido en la unidad. Si haces los ejercicios a medida que avanzas, asimilarás y recordarás mejor los conceptos, y tu inglés será más fluido. Cada ejercicio indica con un símbolo qué habilidad vas a practicar con él.

 GRAMÁTICA
Aplica las nuevas reglas en distintos contextos.

LECTURA
Analiza ejemplos del idioma en textos reales en inglés.

ESCUCHA
Comprueba tu comprensión del inglés hablado.

 VOCABULARIO
Consolida tu comprensión del vocabulario clave.

 CONVERSACIÓN
Compara tu dicción con los audios de muestra.

Número de módulo
Cada módulo tiene su propio número, para que te sea fácil localizar las respuestas y el audio correspondiente.

Instrucciones En cada ejercicio tienes unas breves instrucciones que te dicen qué debes hacer.

13.10 COMPLETA LOS ESPACIOS CON LA FORMA CORRECTA DEL VERBO

 He _finishes_ (finish) work at 5 o'clock.

Respuesta de ejemplo La primera respuesta ya está escrita, para que entiendas mejor el ejercicio.

① Lucia _____ (wake) up at 7am.

② I _____ (get) up at 7:30am.

③ Ethan _____ (go) to work at 5am.

④ You _____ (leave) work at 5pm.

⑤ Shona _____ (watch) TV in the evening.

Espacio para escribir
Es útil que escribas las respuestas en el libro, pues te servirán para repasar lo aprendido.

Ayuda gráfica
Las ilustraciones te ayudan a entender los ejercicios.

Audio de apoyo Este símbolo indica que las respuestas a los ejercicios están disponibles en grabaciones de audio. Escúchalas tras completar el ejercicio.

29.11 LEE LAS FRASES EN VOZ ALTA, Y COMPLETA LOS ESPACIOS

Has Milo got a washing machine?
No, _he hasn't_

① Has she got a toaster?
Yes, _____

② Has the house got a dining room?
Yes, _____

③ Have they got a new refrigerator?
No, _____

④ Has it got a large kitchen?
No, _____

Ejercicios de escucha Este símbolo te avisa de que debes escuchar el audio para poder responder a las preguntas.

45.12 ESCUCHA EL AUDIO Y MARCA QUIÉN ES BUENO O MALO EN CADA ACTIVIDAD

Good at ✓ Bad at ☐   ① Good at ☐ Bad at ☐   ③ Good at ☐ Bad at ☐   ④ Good at ☐ Bad at ☐
② Good at ☐ Bad at ☐

Ejercicio de conversación
Este símbolo indica que debes decir las respuestas en voz alta y compararlas a continuación con su audio correspondiente.

Audio

English for Everyone incorpora abundantes materiales en audio. Te recomendamos que los utilices al máximo, pues te ayudarán a mejorar tu comprensión del inglés hablado y a lograr una pronunciación y un acento más naturales. Escucha cada audio tantas veces como quieras. Páusalo y vuelve atrás en los pasajes que te resulten difíciles, hasta que estés seguro de que has entendido bien lo que se dice.

EJERCICIOS DE ESCUCHA
Este símbolo indica que debes escuchar el audio para poder responder a las preguntas.

AUDIO DE APOYO
Este símbolo indica que dispones de audios adicionales que puedes escuchar tras completar el módulo.

AUDIO GRATUITO
web y app
www.dkefe.com

Mide tu progreso

El curso está pensado para que te sea fácil comprobar tu progreso, e incluye para ello resúmenes de lo aprendido y módulos de repaso. Se incluyen las respuestas de todos los ejercicios, con lo que podrás ver si has entendido correctamente cada apartado.

Checklist Cada unidad termina con un recuadro en el que podrás marcar las habilidades que hayas aprendido.

08 ✓ CHECKLIST

| ⚙ "These" y "those" ☐ | **Aa** Pertenencias ☐ | ♣ Usar determinantes y pronombres ☐ |

Módulos de repaso Al final de cada grupo de unidades tienes un módulo de repaso en el que se resumen con más detalle los aspectos aprendidos en las páginas precedentes.

Casillas de verificación Marca las casillas de los puntos con los que te sientas seguro. Vuelve a repasar los que te hayan resultado más difíciles.

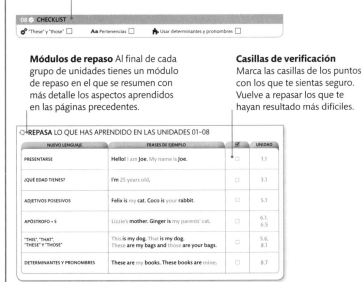

Respuestas Tienes las respuestas de todos los ejercicios al final del libro.

Número de ejercicio Para que las localices más fácilmente, las respuestas indican el número del ejercicio.

Audio Este símbolo indica que puedes escuchar el audio de las respuestas.

01 Presentarse

Puedes saludar a otras personas diciéndoles: "Hello!" o "Hi!". Preséntate con la expresión: "I am". A veces tendrás que deletrear tu nombre.

⚙️ **Lenguaje** Usar "to be" con nombres
Aa Vocabulario Nombres y letras
🧩 **Habilidad** Decir tu nombre

1.1 PUNTO CLAVE DECIR TU NOMBRE

Hay varias formas de saludar y presentarse.

Este saludo puede ser formal o informal.

Hello! I am Lyla.

Puedes usar "I am" y añadir tu nombre.

Este es un saludo informal. Suele usarse en conversaciones casuales.

Hi! My name is Joe.

También puedes usar "My name is" y añadir tu nombre para presentarte.

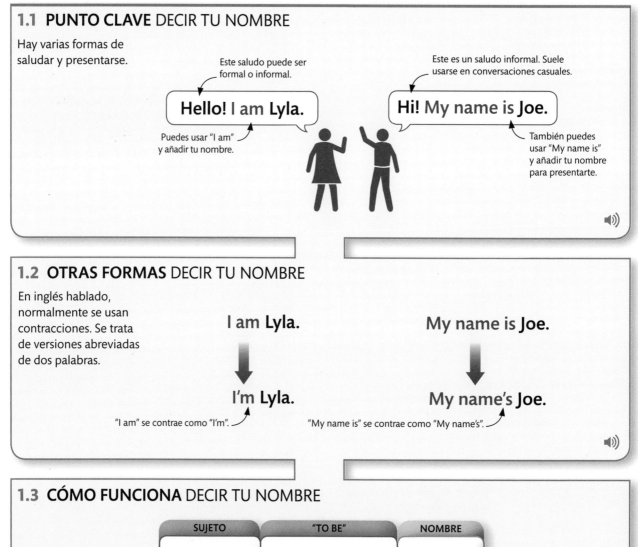

🔊

1.2 OTRAS FORMAS DECIR TU NOMBRE

En inglés hablado, normalmente se usan contracciones. Se trata de versiones abreviadas de dos palabras.

I am Lyla.

⬇️

I'm Lyla.

"I am" se contrae como "I'm".

My name is Joe.

⬇️

My name's Joe.

"My name is" se contrae como "My name's".

🔊

1.3 CÓMO FUNCIONA DECIR TU NOMBRE

SUJETO	"TO BE"	NOMBRE
My name	is	Lyla.
I	am	

Escribe el nombre con mayúscula inicial.

1.4 VUELVE A ESCRIBIR CADA FRASE, UTILIZANDO LA CONTRACCIÓN

> My name is Jack.
> _My name's Jack._

1 I am Charlotte.

_____

2 My name is Una.

_____

3 My name is Simone.

_____

4 I am Carlos.

_____

5 I am Juan.

_____

6 My name is Miriam.

_____

7 I am Sarah.

_____

🔊

1.5 ESCUCHA EL AUDIO Y NUMERA LAS PERSONAS EN EL ORDEN EN QUE HABLAN

A ☐ Charlie

B 1 Katherine

C ☐ JOSEPH

D ☐ Ruby

E ☐ Elliot

F ☐ Oliver

1.6 USA EL DIAGRAMA PARA CREAR 12 FRASES CORRECTAS Y DILAS EN VOZ ALTA.

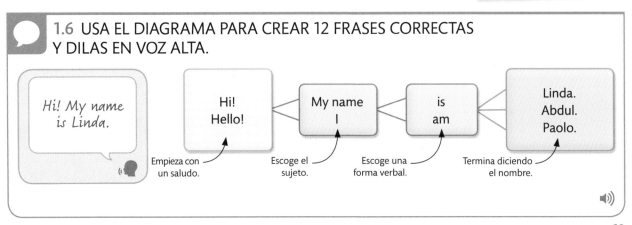

Hi! My name is Linda.

| Hi! Hello! | My name / I | is / am | Linda. Abdul. Paolo. |

Empieza con un saludo.

Escoge el sujeto.

Escoge una forma verbal.

Termina diciendo el nombre.

🔊

1.7 **PUNTO CLAVE** DELETREAR TU NOMBRE

How do you spell your first name?

Así se le pide a alguien
que deletree su nombre.

My name's Jacob, J-A-C-O-B.

Se dice cada letra una a una.

How do you spell your last name?

Así se le pide a alguien que
deletree su apellido.

Williams, W-I-L-L-I-A-M-S.

How do you spell your full name?

Esto es, tu nombre
y tu apellido.

J-A-C-O-B W-I-L-L-I-A-M-S.

1.8 **PRONUNCIACIÓN** EL ABECEDARIO

Escucha cómo se pronuncian las letras
en inglés.

Aa Bb Cc Dd Ee Ff Gg Hh Ii
Jj Kk Ll Mm Nn Oo Pp Qq
Rr Ss Tt Uu Vv Ww Xx Yy Zz

1.9 ESCUCHA EN EL AUDIO A PERSONAS QUE DELETREAN SU NOMBRE. ESCRIBE LAS LETRAS

J-A-C-K L-O-R-D

1. ______________________
2. ______________________
3. ______________________
4. ______________________
5. ______________________
6. ______________________
7. ______________________
8. ______________________
9. ______________________

1.10 DELETREA EL NOMBRE DE CADA PERSONA Y LEE LAS FRASES EN VOZ ALTA

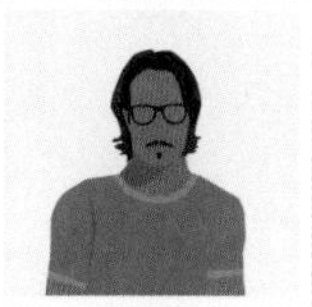

My name is Gabriel,
G-A-B-R-I-E-L.

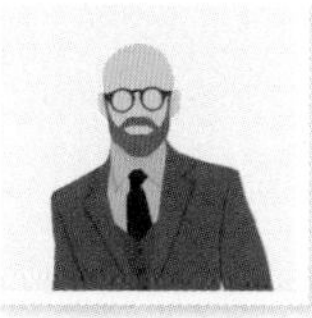

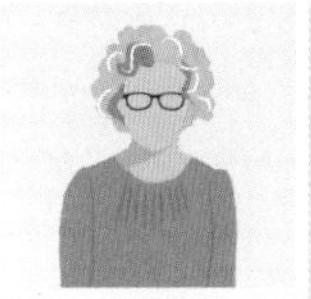

1.

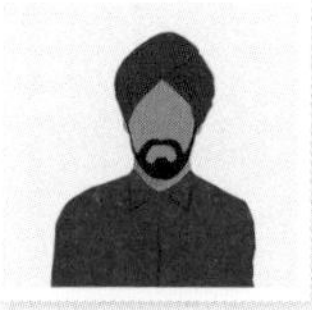

My last name is Bashir,
____

2.

I am Ben James,
____

3.

My name's Molly,
____

4.

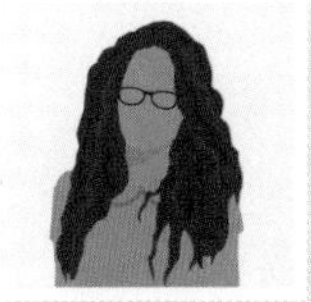

My last name's Lopez,
____

5.

I'm Nadiya Latif,
____

01 CHECKLIST

Usar "to be" con nombres ☐ | **Aa** Nombres y letras ☐ | Decir tu nombre ☐

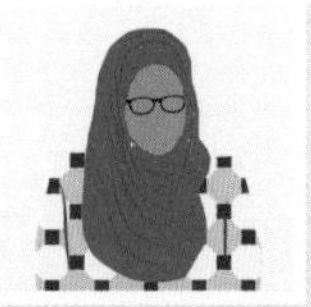

2.1 PAÍSES

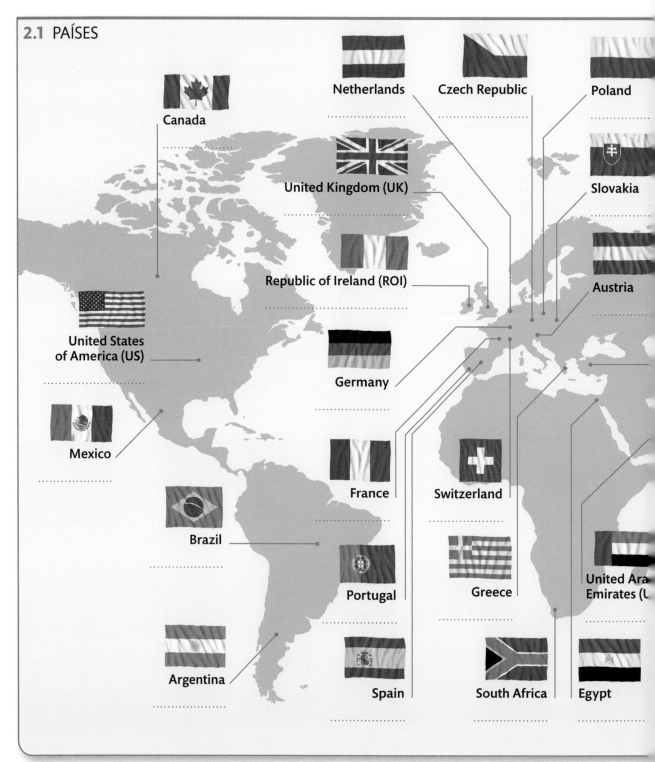

Netherlands

Czech Republic

Poland

Canada

United Kingdom (UK)

Slovakia

Republic of Ireland (ROI)

Austria

United States
of America (US)

Germany

Mexico

France   Switzerland

Brazil

Portugal   Greece

United Ara
Emirates (L

Argentina

Spain   South Africa   Egypt

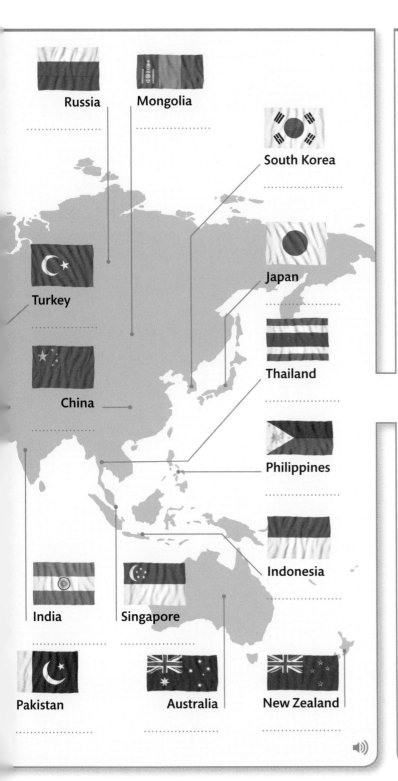

Russia

Mongolia

South Korea

Japan

Turkey

Thailand

China

Philippines

Indonesia

India

Singapore

Pakistan

Australia

New Zealand

USA	⟹	American
Canada	⟹	Canadian
Mexico	⟹	Mexican
Brazil	⟹	Brazilian
Argentina	⟹	Argentinian
UK	⟹	British
France	⟹	French
Russia	⟹	Russian
Spain	⟹	Spanish
Portugal	⟹	Portuguese
Poland	⟹	Polish
Greece	⟹	Greek
Turkey	⟹	Turkish
Egypt	⟹	Egyptian
China	⟹	Chinese
Japan	⟹	Japanese
India	⟹	Indian
Pakistan	⟹	Pakistani
Mongolia	⟹	Mongolian
Australia	⟹	Australian
Germany	⟹	German
Switzerland	⟹	Swiss
Austria	⟹	Austrian

03 Hablar de ti

Es útil saber cómo decir tu edad y de dónde eres.
Para ello, puedes utilizar el verbo "to be".

⚙ **Lenguaje** "To be" con edades y nacionalidades
Aa Vocabulario Números y nacionalidades
🧩 **Habilidad** Hablar de ti

3.1 PUNTO CLAVE DECIR TU EDAD

Utiliza el verbo "to be"
para decir tu edad.

How old are you?

I am 25 years old.

El verbo "to be" cambia
con el sujeto.

3.2 MÁS EJEMPLOS DECIR TU EDAD

Ruby is **seven years old.**

 I'm **44 today.**

Izzy and Chloe are **13.**

My grandma is **92 years old.**

3.3 CÓMO FUNCIONA DECIR TU EDAD

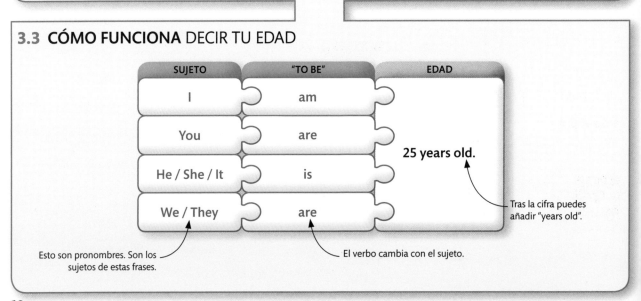

SUJETO	"TO BE"	EDAD
I	am	
You	are	25 years old.
He / She / It	is	
We / They	are	

Esto son pronombres. Son los
sujetos de estas frases.

El verbo cambia con el sujeto.

Tras la cifra puedes
añadir "years old".

3.4 VOCABULARIO NÚMEROS

1 one	**2** two	**3** three	**4** four	**5** five	**6** six
7 seven	**8** eight	**9** nine	**10** ten	**11** eleven	**12** twelve
13 thirteen	**14** fourteen	**15** fifteen	**16** sixteen	**17** seventeen	**18** eighteen
19 nineteen	**20** twenty	**21** twenty-one	**22** twenty-two	**30** thirty	**40** forty
50 fifty	**60** sixty	**70** seventy	**80** eighty	**90** ninety	**100** one hundred

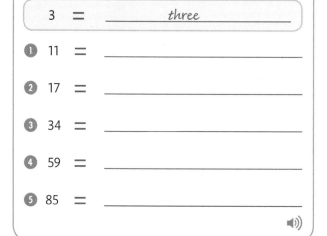

Aa 3.5 ESCRIBE LOS NÚMEROS EN PALABRAS

3 = _three_

① 11 = _____

② 17 = _____

③ 34 = _____

④ 59 = _____

⑤ 85 = _____

3.6 COMPLETA LOS ESPACIOS CON LA FORMA CORRECTA DE "TO BE"

Michael ___is___ 32 years old.

① Theo _____ 45 years old.

② Madison _____ 27 years old.

③ Jeremy and Tanya _____ 90 years old.

④ We _____ 29 years old.

⑤ I _____ 34 years old.

3.7 PRONUNCIACIÓN NÚMEROS QUE SUENAN DE MODO SIMILAR

Es importante acentuar la sílaba correcta en estos números.

Acentúa la última sílaba.

Acentúa la primera sílaba.

13	**Thirteen**	30	**Thirty**
14	**Fourteen**	40	**Forty**
15	**Fifteen**	50	**Fifty**
16	**Sixteen**	60	**Sixty**
17	**Seventeen**	70	**Seventy**
18	**Eighteen**	80	**Eighty**
19	**Nineteen**	90	**Ninety**

3.8 ESCUCHA EL AUDIO Y MARCA LAS EDADES CORRECTAS

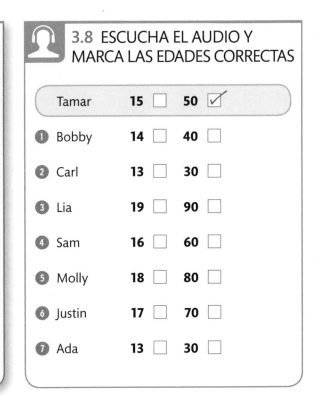

Tamar	15 ☐	50 ☑
❶ Bobby	14 ☐	40 ☐
❷ Carl	13 ☐	30 ☐
❸ Lia	19 ☐	90 ☐
❹ Sam	16 ☐	60 ☐
❺ Molly	18 ☐	80 ☐
❻ Justin	17 ☐	70 ☐
❼ Ada	13 ☐	30 ☐

3.9 PUNTO CLAVE DECIR DE DÓNDE ERES

Hay diferentes maneras de decir de dónde eres.

Para preguntar el lugar utilizamos la palabra "where".

Recuerda que "to be" cambia con el sujeto.

Así se indica el país de donde eres.

Para indicar la nacionalidad se utiliza un adjetivo.

Where are you from?

I am from Spain.

What nationality are you?

I'm Spanish.

3.10 MÁS EJEMPLOS DECIR DE DÓNDE ERES

I am Dutch.

We are Italian.

I'm from Switzerland.

3.11 CÓMO FUNCIONA DECIR DE DÓNDE ERES

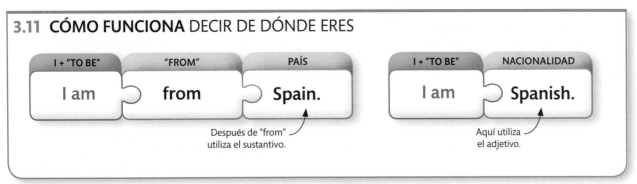

I + "TO BE"	"FROM"	PAÍS
I am	from	Spain.

Después de "from" utiliza el sustantivo.

I + "TO BE"	NACIONALIDAD
I am	Spanish.

Aquí utiliza el adjetivo.

Aa 3.12 CONECTA CADA BANDERA CON SU PAÍS

Japan

UK

France

US

3.13 ESCRIBE LA NACIONALIDAD DE CADA PAÍS

Italy = _Italian_

1 Spain = _____

2 Germany = _____

3 Canada = _____

4 America = _____

5 Australia = _____

6 China = _____

3.14 USA EL DIAGRAMA PARA CREAR 12 FRASES CORRECTAS Y DILAS EN VOZ ALTA

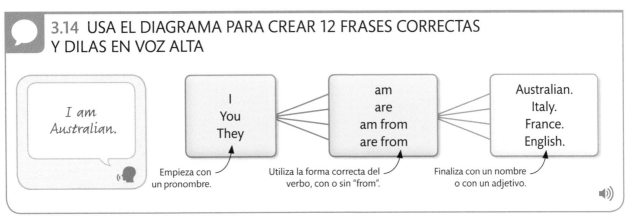

I am Australian.

I You They	am are am from are from	Australian. Italy. France. English.

Empieza con un pronombre.

Utiliza la forma correcta del verbo, con o sin "from".

Finaliza con un nombre o con un adjetivo.

---

03 ✓ CHECKLIST

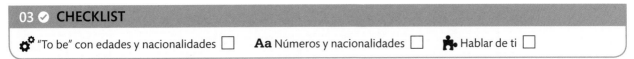

⚙ "To be" con edades y nacionalidades ☐   Aa Números y nacionalidades ☐   🧩 Hablar de ti ☐

4.1 LA FAMILIA DE PABLO

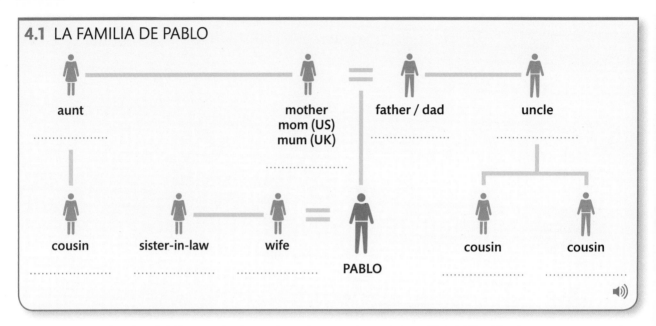

aunt

mother
mom (US)
mum (UK)

father / dad

uncle

cousin

sister-in-law

wife

PABLO

cousin

cousin

4.2 LA FAMILIA DE MARY

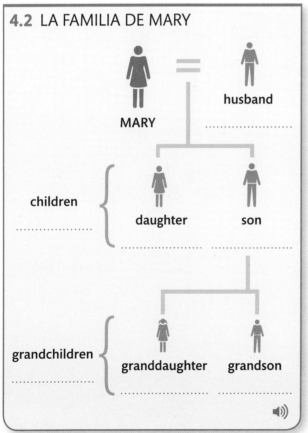

MARY

husband

children

daughter

son

grandchildren

granddaughter

grandson

4.3 LA FAMILIA DE SARAH

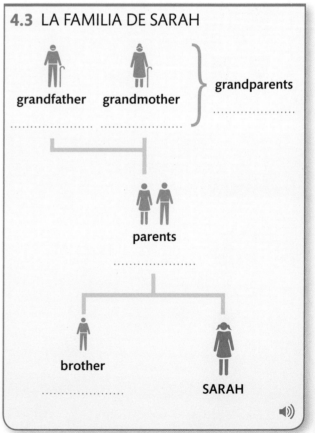

grandfather

grandmother

grandparents

parents

brother

SARAH

4.4 LA FAMILIA DE DAN

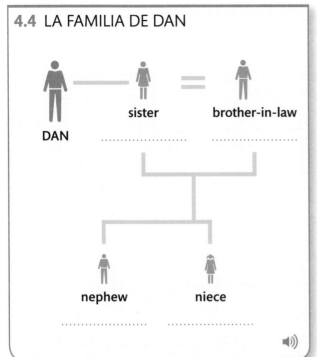

DAN — sister = brother-in-law

nephew .... niece ....

4.5 LA FAMILIA DE HARRY

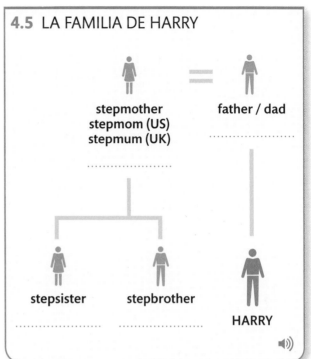

stepmother
stepmom (US)
stepmum (UK) = father / dad

stepsister .... stepbrother ....

HARRY

4.6 MASCOTAS Y ANIMALES DOMÉSTICOS

cat ....   dog ....   rabbit ....   hamster ....   guinea pig ....

fish ....   parrot ....   tortoise ....   snake ....   donkey ....

pig ....   chicken ....   sheep ....   horse ....   cow ....

05 Tus cosas

Los adjetivos posesivos nos indican a quién le pertenece algo (una mascota, por ejemplo). "This" y "that" son determinantes. Señalan a una persona o un objeto concretos.

⚙ **Lenguaje** Adjetivos posesivos, "this" y "that"
Aa Vocabulario Animales y familia
🧩 **Habilidad** Hablar de a quién pertenecen las cosas

5.1 PUNTO CLAVE ADJETIVOS POSESIVOS

Los adjetivos posesivos se usan delante del nombre.
Cambian según si el propietario es singular, plural, masculino o femenino, la persona con la que hablas o tú mismo.

Felix is my cat.

El gato es mío.

Buster is her dog.
El perro pertenece a una mujer.

Rachel is our daughter.
Nosotros somos sus padres.

Coco is your rabbit.
El conejo es tuyo.

Polly is his parrot.
El loro pertenece a un hombre.

John is their son.
Ellos son sus padres.

🔊

5.2 CÓMO FUNCIONA ADJETIVOS POSESIVOS

I	you	he	she	it	we	they
⬇	⬇	⬇	⬇	⬇	⬇	⬇
my	your	his	her	its	our	their
⬇	⬇	⬇	⬇	⬇	⬇	⬇
my cat	your rabbit	his wife	her sister	its ball	our horse	their son

🔊

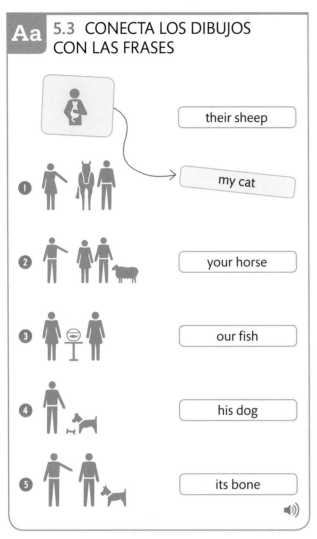

Aa 5.3 CONECTA LOS DIBUJOS CON LAS FRASES

their sheep

my cat

your horse

our fish

his dog

its bone

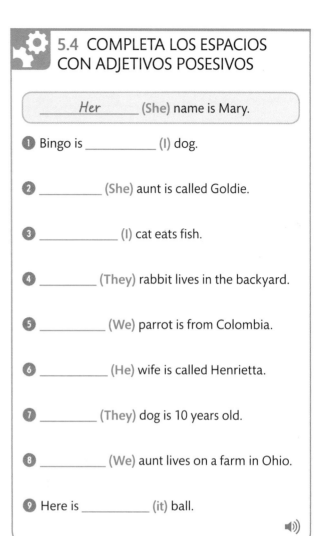

5.4 COMPLETA LOS ESPACIOS CON ADJETIVOS POSESIVOS

_____Her_____ (She) name is Mary.

1 Bingo is _____ (I) dog.

2 _____ (She) aunt is called Goldie.

3 _____ (I) cat eats fish.

4 _____ (They) rabbit lives in the backyard.

5 _____ (We) parrot is from Colombia.

6 _____ (He) wife is called Henrietta.

7 _____ (They) dog is 10 years old.

8 _____ (We) aunt lives on a farm in Ohio.

9 Here is _____ (it) ball.

5.5 VUELVE A ESCRIBIR LAS FRASES CORRIGIENDO LOS ERRORES

Nick **are** my brother.
Nick is my brother.

1 Farida **are** their sister.

2 Duke **am** our dog.

3 Daisy **are** her mother.

4 They **is** his grandparents.

5 It **am** our horse.

6 John **am** our cousin.

7 I **are** Daisy's daughter.

8 You **is** my friend.

5.6 PUNTO CLAVE "THIS" Y "THAT"

"This" y "that" se llaman determinantes. Señalan un objeto específico del que se quiere hablar. Utiliza "this" para algo cercano a ti. Utiliza "that" para algo que está más lejos.

This is my dog.

El perro está cerca de ti.

That is my dog.

El perro está lejos de ti.

5.7 MÁS EJEMPLOS "THIS" Y "THAT"

This is your rabbit.

This is her horse.

This is its bed.

That is your rabbit.

That is her horse.

That is its bed.

5.8 COMPLETA LOS ESPACIOS USANDO "THIS" O "THAT"

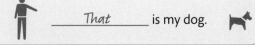
_____That_____ is my dog.

❸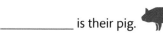
_____ is their pig.

❶
_____ is her horse.

❹
_____ is his cow.

❷
_____ is our rabbit.

❺
_____ is your fish.

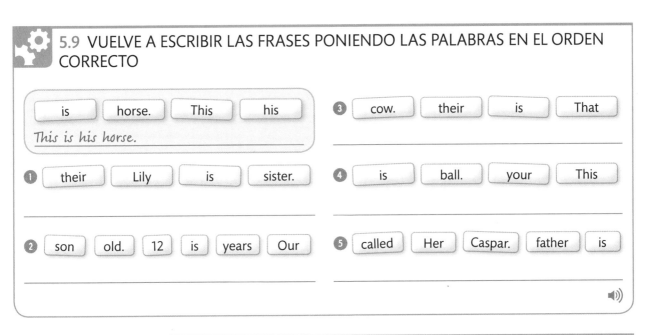

5.9 VUELVE A ESCRIBIR LAS FRASES PONIENDO LAS PALABRAS EN EL ORDEN CORRECTO

| is | horse. | This | his |

This is his horse.

3 | cow. | their | is | That |

_____

1 | their | Lily | is | sister. |

_____

4 | is | ball. | your | This |

_____

2 | son | old. | 12 | is | years | Our |

_____

5 | called | Her | Caspar. | father | is |

_____

5.10 ESCUCHA EL AUDIO Y LUEGO NUMERA LAS IMÁGENES EN EL ORDEN EN QUE SE DESCRIBEN

A ☐   B [1]   C ☐   D ☐   E ☐

5.11 USA EL DIAGRAMA PARA CREAR 12 FRASES CORRECTAS Y DILAS EN VOZ ALTA

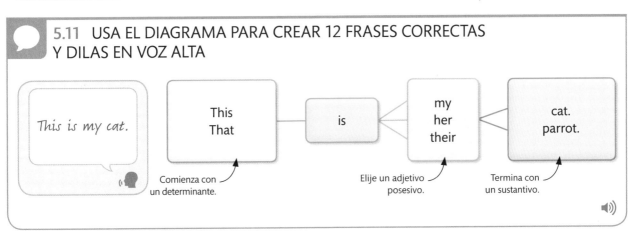

This is my cat.

This / That — is — my / her / their — cat. / parrot.

Comienza con un determinante.

Elije un adjetivo posesivo.

Termina con un sustantivo.

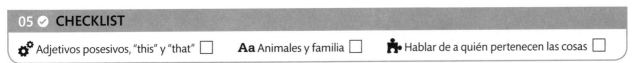

05 ✓ CHECKLIST

⚙ Adjetivos posesivos, "this" y "that" ☐   **Aa** Animales y familia ☐   🧩 Hablar de a quién pertenecen las cosas ☐

06 Uso del apóstrofo

En inglés se puede utilizar el apóstrofo (') para mostrar pertenencia. Se utiliza para mostrar de quién es algo, como una mascota, y para hablar sobre la familia.

⚙️ **Lenguaje** Apóstrofo posesivo
Aa Vocabulario Familia y mascotas
🧩 **Habilidad** Hablar de pertenencia

6.1 PUNTO CLAVE APÓSTROFO CON "S"

Añade un apóstrofo y la letra "s" al final de un sustantivo singular para indicar que el sustantivo que le sigue le pertenece.

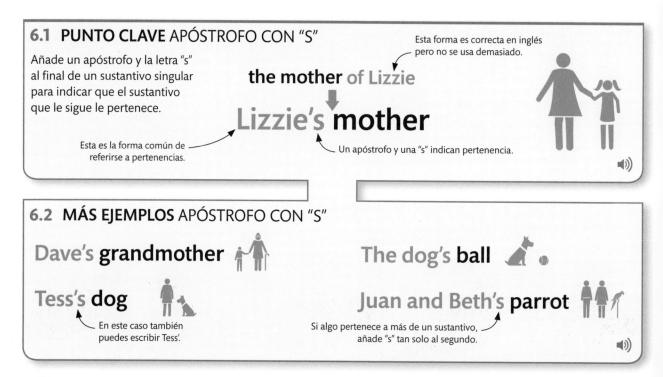

Esta forma es correcta en inglés pero no se usa demasiado.

the mother of Lizzie

Lizzie's mother

Esta es la forma común de referirse a pertenencias.

Un apóstrofo y una "s" indican pertenencia.

6.2 MÁS EJEMPLOS APÓSTROFO CON "S"

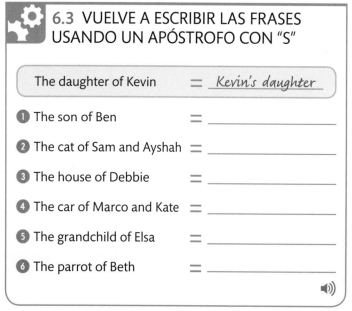

Dave's grandmother

Tess's dog

En este caso también puedes escribir Tess'.

The dog's ball

Juan and Beth's parrot

Si algo pertenece a más de un sustantivo, añade "s" tan solo al segundo.

6.3 VUELVE A ESCRIBIR LAS FRASES USANDO UN APÓSTROFO CON "S"

The daughter of Kevin = *Kevin's daughter*

1 The son of Ben = _____

2 The cat of Sam and Ayshah = _____

3 The house of Debbie = _____

4 The car of Marco and Kate = _____

5 The grandchild of Elsa = _____

6 The parrot of Beth = _____

6.4 ESCUCHA EL AUDIO Y CONECTA LAS PAREJAS

Edith is — Ben's mother.

1 Lucas is → Ben's grandmother.

2 Lily is — Ben's son.

3 Noah is — Ben's sister.

4 Grace is — Ben's brother.

5 Alex is — Ben's father.

6.5 PUNTO CLAVE APÓSTROFOS Y SUSTANTIVOS EN PLURAL

Para indicar pertenencia con un sustantivo en plural, añade el apóstrofo sin la "s".

Ginger is my parents' cat.

Los sustantivos en plural llevan un apóstrofo sin la "s".

6.6 MÁS EJEMPLOS APÓSTROFOS Y SUSTANTIVOS EN PLURAL

This is my cousins' rabbit.

That is his grandparents' house.

Rex is her brothers' dog.

Polly is our children's parrot.

En los nombres plurales no terminados en "s," también debe añadirse "s."

6.7 VUELVE A ESCRIBIR LAS FRASES EN EL ORDEN CORRECTO

| uncle. | Kevin | Sharon's | is |

Kevin is Sharon's uncle.

❶ | Skanda's | is | wife. | Angela |

_____

❷ | snake. | is | my cousins' | That |

_____

❸ | Sue | aunt. | Ella and Mark's | is |

_____

❹ | is | John's | cat. | Ginger |

_____

6.8 DI LAS FRASES EN ALTO COMPLETANDO LOS ESPACIOS

Edith is ___Ben's___ (Ben) grandmother.

❶ Kathy is _____ (Dave) aunt.

❷ Rex is _____ (Noah and Pat) dog.

❸ This is _____ (her cousins) house.

❹ Felix is _____ (the children) cat.

---

06 ✓ CHECKLIST

⚙ Apóstrofo posesivo ☐   **Aa** Familia y mascotas ☐   🧩 Hablar de pertenencia ☐

07 Vocabulario

7.1 OBJETOS COTIDIANOS

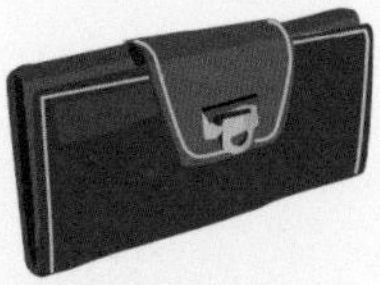

wallet (US)
purse (UK)

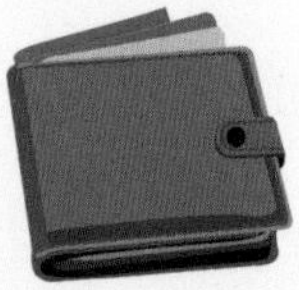

wallet

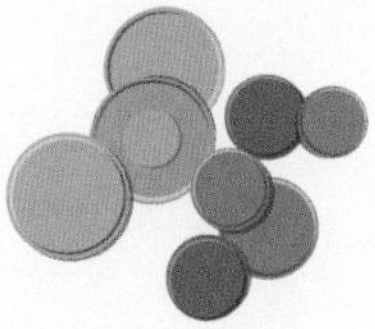

coins

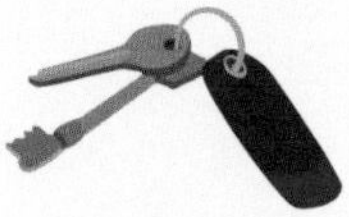

keys

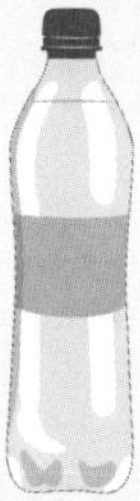

bottle of water

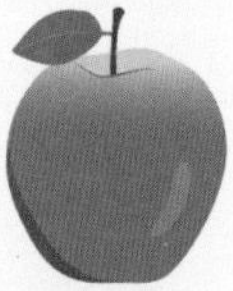

apple

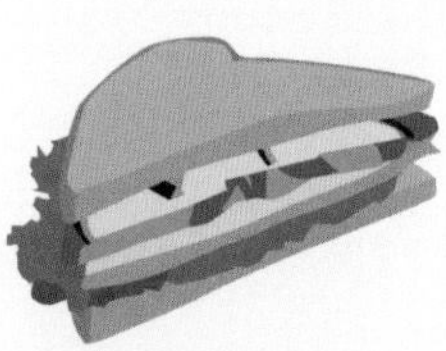

sandwich

cell phone (US)
mobile phone (UK)

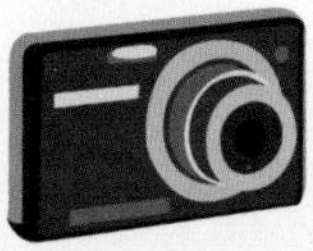

camera

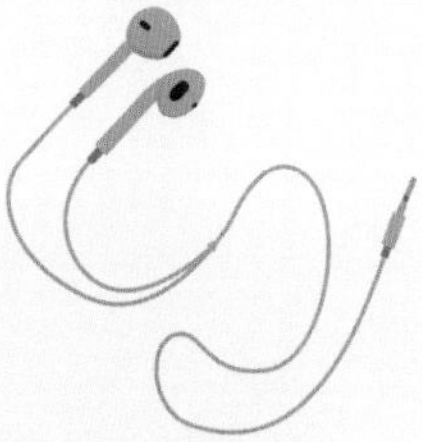

earphones

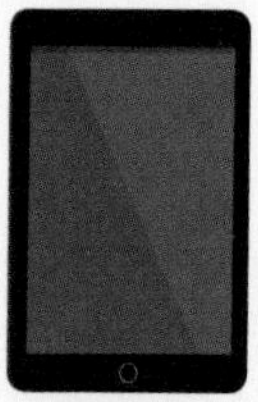

tablet

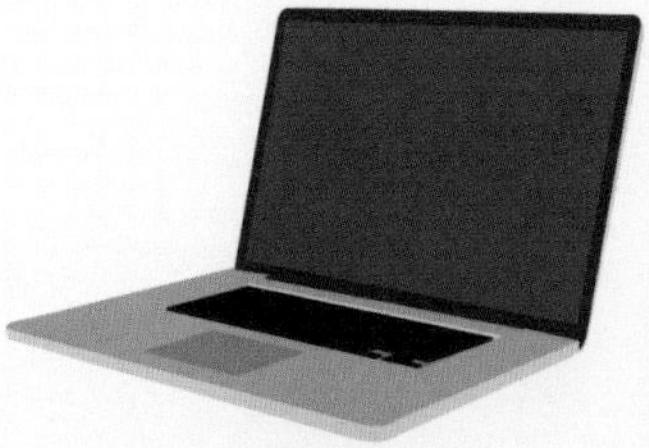

laptop

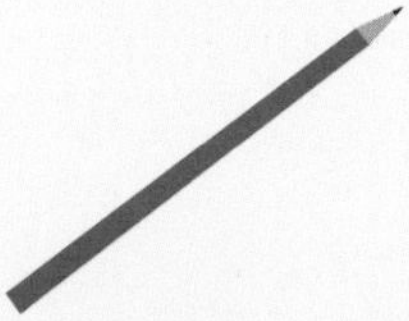

pencil

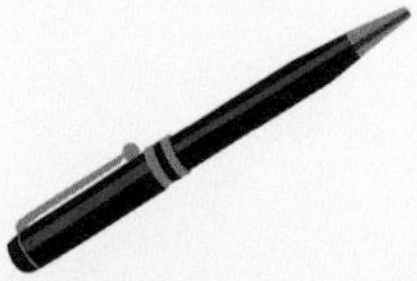

pen

notebook

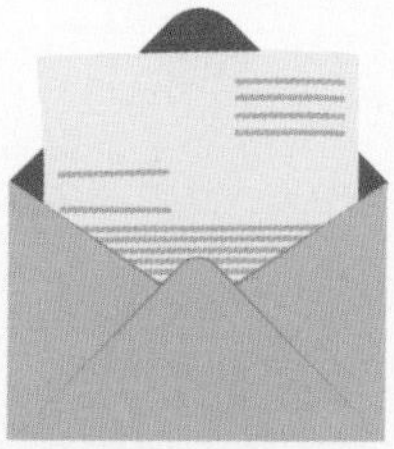

letter

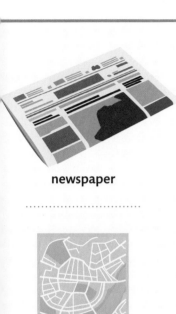
newspaper

magazine

book / novel

dictionary

map

mirror

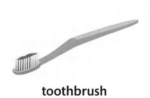
toothbrush

umbrella

hairbrush

planner (US)
diary (UK)

glasses

sunglasses

necklace

watch

passport

ID card

31

08 Hablar de tus cosas

Al referirnos a más de un objeto utilizamos "these" y "those". Para indicar a quién le pertenece algo, podemos utilizar los determinantes o los pronombres posesivos.

⚙ **Lenguaje** "These" y "those"
Aa Vocabulario Pertenencias
🧩 **Habilidad** Usar determinantes y pronombres

8.1 PUNTO CLAVE USAR "THESE" Y "THOSE"

Utiliza "this" para algo que está cerca de ti.

This is my bag.

Utiliza "that" para algo que está lejos de ti.

That is my bag.

"These" es el plural de "this".

These are my bags.

"Those" es el plural de "that".

Those are my bags.

Utiliza también "these" y "those" para diferenciar. Estas cosas pertenecen a una persona.

Esas cosas pertenecen a otra persona.

These are my bags and those are your bags.

8.2 TACHA LA PALABRA INCORRECTA DE CADA FRASE

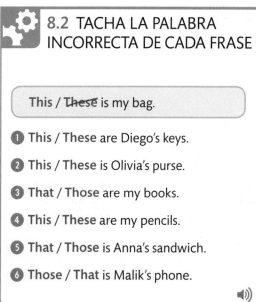

This / ~~These~~ is my bag.

1. This / These are Diego's keys.
2. This / These is Olivia's purse.
3. That / Those are my books.
4. This / These are my pencils.
5. That / Those is Anna's sandwich.
6. Those / That is Malik's phone.

8.3 VUELVE A ESCRIBIR LAS FRASES EN SU OTRA FORMA

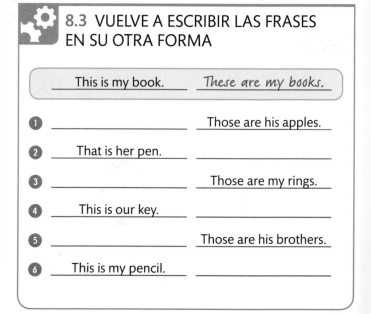

This is my book.	*These are my books.*
1	Those are his apples.
2 That is her pen.	
3	Those are my rings.
4 This is our key.	
5	Those are his brothers.
6 This is my pencil.	

8.4 VOCABULARIO REGLAS PARA FOMAR PLURALES

Para formar el plural de la mayoría de sustantivos, añade una "s".

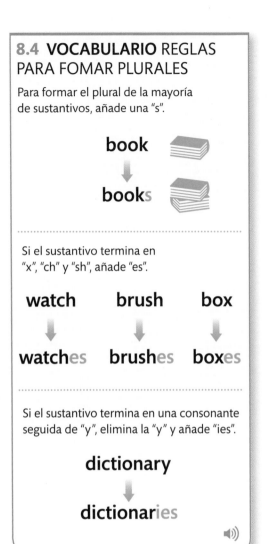

book

↓

books

Si el sustantivo termina en "x", "ch" y "sh", añade "es".

watch   brush   box

↓   ↓   ↓

watches   brushes   boxes

Si el sustantivo termina en una consonante seguida de "y", elimina la "y" y añade "ies".

dictionary

↓

dictionaries

🔊

Aa 8.5 BUSCA OCHO PLURALES EN LA TABLA Y ESCRÍBELOS EN SU GRUPO

```
W A T C H E S O B W O A D
A B P X E I N G A Q E P I
N D E M B R U S H E S P A
N E C K L A C E S A C L R
S A N D W I C H E S I E I
D I C T I O N A R I E S E
B O T T L E S Z I S R E S
P Q I W T I O S Y U R D S
T L E L L S H B N E Y S I
```

PLURALES EN "S"	PLURALES EN "ES"	PLURALES EN "IES"
① _apples_	④ _____	⑦ _____
② _____	⑤ _____	⑧ _____
③ _____	⑥ _____	

🔊

Aa 8.6 ESCRIBE UN PLURAL PARA DESCRIBIR CADA DIBUJO

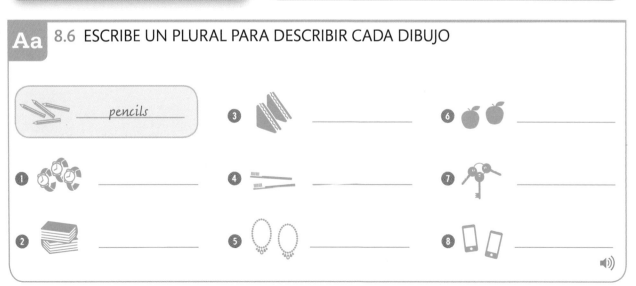

pencils

① _____

② _____

③ _____

④ _____

⑤ _____

⑥ _____

⑦ _____

⑧ _____

🔊

8.7 PUNTO CLAVE DETERMINANTES Y PRONOMBRES

Para explicar de quién es algo puedes utilizar los determinantes o los pronombres posesivos.

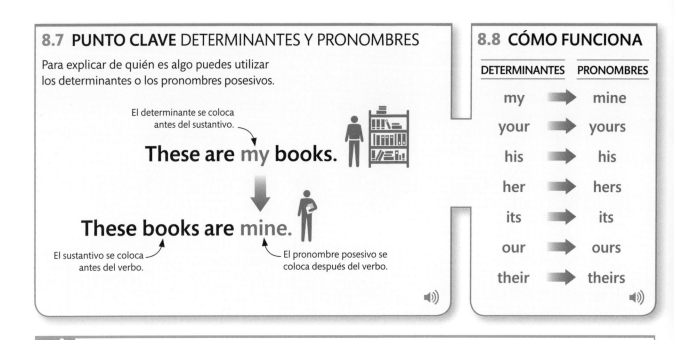

El determinante se coloca antes del sustantivo.

These are my books.

These books are mine.

El sustantivo se coloca antes del verbo.

El pronombre posesivo se coloca después del verbo.

8.8 CÓMO FUNCIONA

DETERMINANTES	PRONOMBRES
my ➡	mine
your ➡	yours
his ➡	his
her ➡	hers
its ➡	its
our ➡	ours
their ➡	theirs

8.9 COMPLETA LOS ESPACIOS Y ESCRIBE CADA FRASE DE OTRAS DOS MANERAS

These are Aman's books.	*These are his books.*	*These books are his.*
❶ This is Leesa's laptop.		
❷ Those are Una and Ben's keys.		
❸ These are Jo's and my passports.		
❹ That is John's brush.		

8.10 ESCUCHA EL AUDIO Y ESCRIBE CADA NOMBRE EN EL GRUPO CORRECTO

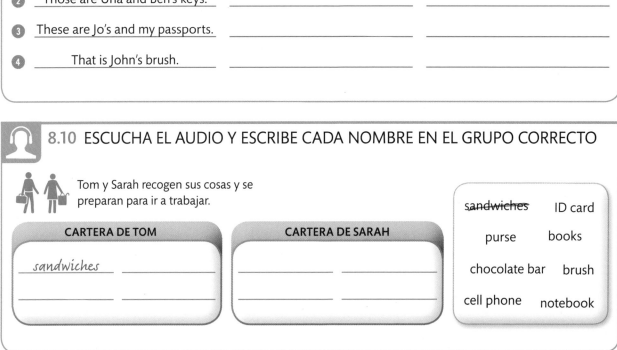

Tom y Sarah recogen sus cosas y se preparan para ir a trabajar.

CARTERA DE TOM	CARTERA DE SARAH
sandwiches	

~~sandwiches~~ ID card

purse books

chocolate bar brush

cell phone notebook

8.11 USA EL DIAGRAMA PARA CREAR 12 FRASES CORRECTAS Y DILAS EN VOZ ALTA

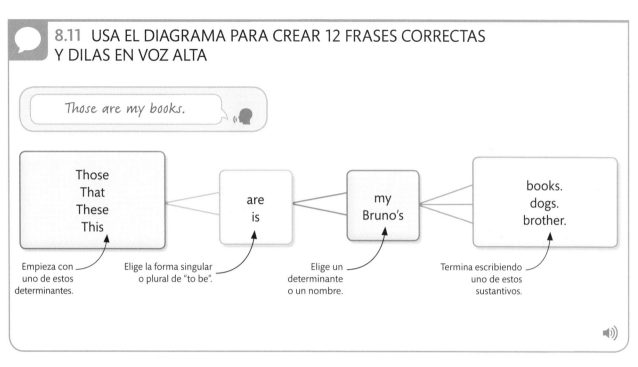

Those are my books.

| Those / That / These / This | are / is | my / Bruno's | books. / dogs. / brother. |

Empieza con uno de estos determinantes.

Elige la forma singular o plural de "to be".

Elige un determinante o un nombre.

Termina escribiendo uno de estos sustantivos.

---

08 ✓ CHECKLIST

⚙ "These" y "those" ☐　　　**Aa** Pertenencias ☐　　　🧩 Usar determinantes y pronombres ☐

♻ REPASA LO QUE HAS APRENDIDO EN LAS UNIDADES 01–08

NUEVO LENGUAJE	FRASES DE EJEMPLO	☑	UNIDAD
PRESENTARSE	Hello! I am Joe. My name is Joe.	☐	1.1
¿QUÉ EDAD TIENES?	I'm 25 years old.	☐	3.1
ADJETIVOS POSESIVOS	Felix is my cat. Coco is your rabbit.	☐	5.1
APÓSTROFO + S	Lizzie's mother. Ginger is my parents' cat.	☐	6.1, 6.5
"THIS", "THAT", "THESE" Y "THOSE"	This is my dog. That is my dog. These are my bags and those are your bags.	☐	5.6, 8.1
DETERMINANTES Y PRONOMBRES	These are my books. These books are mine.	☐	8.7

Vocabulario

9.1 TRABAJOS

cleaner

driver

sales assistant

hairdresser

chef

gardener

vet

actor

doctor

nurse

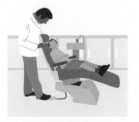

dentist

police officer

fire fighter

farmer

construction worker (US)
builder (UK)

artist

receptionist

mechanic

engineer

scientist

teacher

businesswoman

businessman

waiter

waitress

electrician

pilot

judge

9.2 PLURALES

La mayoría de los sustantivos que se refieren a personas y trabajos forman el plural añadiendo "-s" o "-es".

driver → drivers

waitress → waitresses

Los sustantivos acabados en "man" forman el plural cambiando esta terminación por "men".

man → men

woman → women

businessman → businessmen

businesswoman → businesswomen

Los sustantivos integrados por dos palabras forman el plural modificando tan solo la segunda.

police officer → police officers

37

10 Hablar de tu trabajo

Para describir tu trabajo puedes utilizar el verbo "to be". El verbo "to work" puede dar más información acerca de dónde trabajas y con quién.

⚙ **Lenguaje** Usar "I am" para tu trabajo
Aa Vocabulario Trabajos y lugares de trabajo
🧩 **Habilidad** Describir tu trabajo

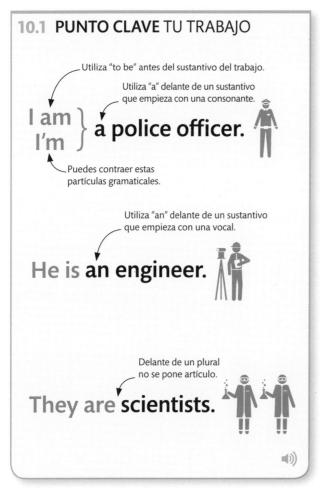

10.1 PUNTO CLAVE TU TRABAJO

Utiliza "to be" antes del sustantivo del trabajo.

Utiliza "a" delante de un sustantivo que empieza con una consonante.

I am ⎱
I'm ⎰ **a police officer.**

Puedes contraer estas partículas gramaticales.

Utiliza "an" delante de un sustantivo que empieza con una vocal.

He is an engineer.

Delante de un plural no se pone artículo.

They are scientists.

🔊))

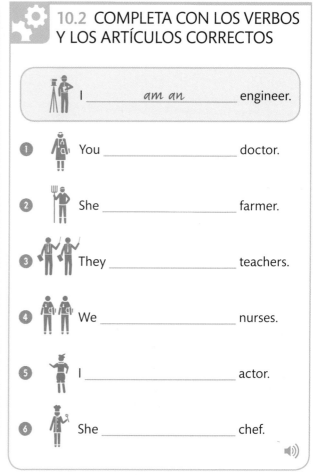

10.2 COMPLETA CON LOS VERBOS Y LOS ARTÍCULOS CORRECTOS

I _____ am an _____ engineer.

1 You _____ doctor.

2 She _____ farmer.

3 They _____ teachers.

4 We _____ nurses.

5 I _____ actor.

6 She _____ chef.

🔊))

10.3 TACHA LA PALABRA INCORRECTA DE CADA FRASE

They are / ~~is~~ farmers.

1 You are / is a driver.

2 I am / is a mechanic.

3 He is / are a vet.

4 We am / are sales assistants.

5 They is / are businesswomen.

6 She is / are a waitress.

7 We is / are receptionists.

8 She is / are a gardener.

🔊))

10.4 VOCABULARIO LUGARES DE TRABAJO

farm

office

theater (US)
theatre (UK)

school

laboratory

restaurant

construction site

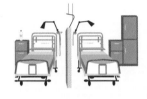

hospital

Aa 10.5 CONECTA LOS TRABAJOS Y LOS LUGARES DE TRABAJO

businessman	farm
1 nurse	restaurant
2 farmer	office
3 scientist	hospital
4 waiter	laboratory
5 teacher	construction site
6 builder	school
7 doctor	theater
8 actor	restaurant
9 chef	hospital

10.6 PUNTO CLAVE INTERIOR/EXTERIOR

Utiliza "inside" para trabajos dentro de un edificio.

 A scientist works inside.

Utiliza "outside" para trabajos al aire libre.

 A farmer works outside.

Aa 10.7 MARCA LAS RESPUESTAS CORRECTAS

A hairdresser works outside.	True ☐	False ✓
1 A driver works outside.	True ☐	False ☐
2 A chef works outside.	True ☐	False ☐
3 A doctor works inside.	True ☐	False ☐
4 A gardener works outside.	True ☐	False ☐

10.8 PUNTO CLAVE USAR "WORK IN" Y "WORK ON"

Utiliza "work in" para referirte a la mayoría de lugares de trabajo.

I work in a hospital.

I work on a farm. I work on construction sites.

Utiliza "work on" para referirte a granjas y obras de construcción.

10.9 ESCUCHA EL AUDIO Y LUEGO NUMERA LAS IMÁGENES EN EL ORDEN EN QUE SE DESCRIBEN

A ☐

C 1

E ☐

B ☐

D ☐

F ☐

10.10 ESCRIBE DOS FRASES PARA DESCRIBIR CADA DIBUJO

Tom _is a farmer._
He works on a farm.

② We _____

_____

④ He _____

_____

① She _____

_____

③ You _____

_____

⑤ Chloe _____

_____

10.11 PUNTO CLAVE "WORK WITH"

Utiliza "work with" seguido de un sustantivo relacionado con tu trabajo.

I work with **animals.**

10.12 VOCABULARIO "WORK WITH"

animals

children

patients

plants

food

people

10.13 ESCUCHA EL AUDIO Y CONECTA PERSONAS Y TRABAJOS

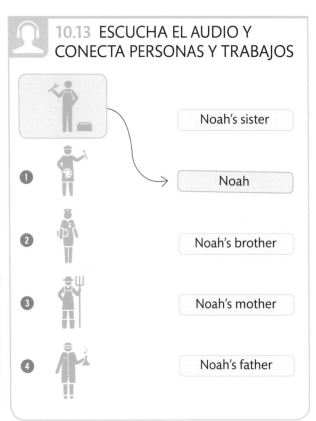

Noah's sister

❶   Noah

Noah's brother

❷

Noah's mother

❸

Noah's father

❹

10.14 DI LAS FRASES EN VOZ ALTA, COMPLETANDO LOS ESPACIOS

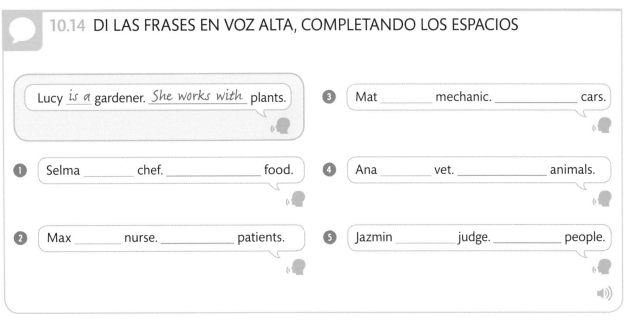

Lucy _is a_ gardener. _She works with_ plants.

❶ Selma _____ chef. _____ food.

❷ Max _____ nurse. _____ patients.

❸ Mat _____ mechanic. _____ cars.

❹ Ana _____ vet. _____ animals.

❺ Jazmin _____ judge. _____ people.

11 Decir la hora

En inglés, hay dos maneras de decir la hora. Puedes utilizar las horas y los minutos, o puedes decir primero los minutos y después la relación que se establece con la hora.

⚙ **Lenguaje** Horas del día
Aa Vocabulario Palabras para indicar la hora
🧩 **Habilidad** Decir la hora

11.1 PUNTO CLAVE DECIR LA HORA

Utiliza el verbo "to be" para indicar y para preguntar la hora en inglés.

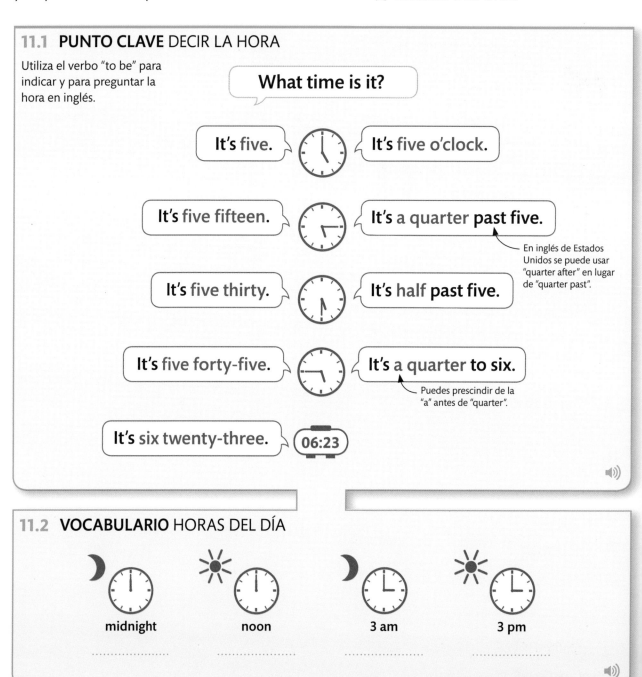

What time is it?

It's five. It's five o'clock.

It's five fifteen. It's a quarter **past five.**

En inglés de Estados Unidos se puede usar "quarter after" en lugar de "quarter past".

It's five thirty. It's half **past five.**

It's five forty-five. It's a quarter **to six.**

Puedes prescindir de la "a" antes de "quarter".

It's six twenty-three. 06:23

11.2 VOCABULARIO HORAS DEL DÍA

midnight   noon   3 am   3 pm

11.3 CONECTA LOS RELOJES CON LA FRASE CORRECTA

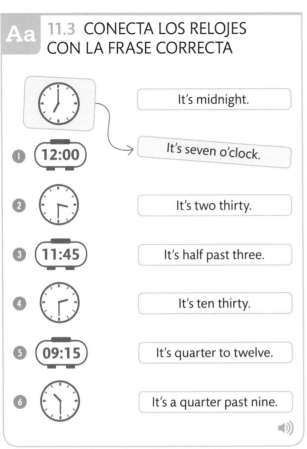

It's midnight.

It's seven o'clock.

It's two thirty.

It's half past three.

It's ten thirty.

It's quarter to twelve.

It's a quarter past nine.

11.5 ESCRIBE LAS HORAS CON NÚMEROS

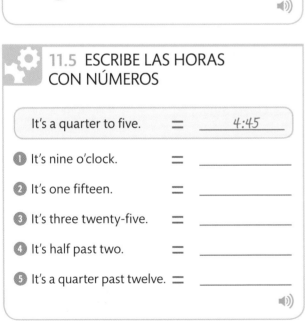

It's a quarter to five. = 4:45

1 It's nine o'clock. = _____

2 It's one fifteen. = _____

3 It's three twenty-five. = _____

4 It's half past two. = _____

5 It's a quarter past twelve. = _____

11.4 ESCUCHA EL AUDIO Y MARCA LAS HORAS QUE OYES

11.6 ESCRIBE LAS HORAS Y LUEGO DILAS EN VOZ ALTA

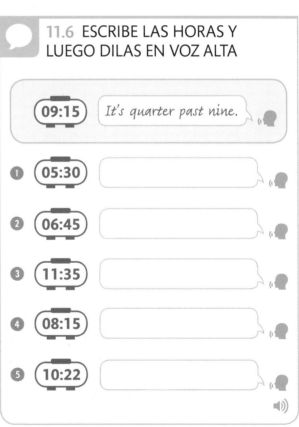

09:15   It's quarter past nine.

1 05:30

2 06:45

3 11:35

4 08:15

5 10:22

12 Vocabulario

Vocabulario

12.1 ACTIVIDADES DIARIAS

wake up

get up

**take a shower (US)
have a shower (UK)**

**take a bath (US)
have a bath (UK)**

brush your hair

**have breakfast /
eat breakfast**

go to work

go to school

buy groceries

go home

cook dinner

**have dinner /
eat dinner**

12.2 HORAS DEL DÍA

day

night

dawn

morning

iron a shirt

get dressed

brush your teeth

wash your face

start work

have lunch /
eat lunch

finish work

leave work

clear the table

do the dishes (US)
wash the dishes (UK)

walk the dog

go to bed

afternoon

dusk

evening

late evening

13 Describir tu jornada

Utiliza el present simple para hablar sobre tus actividades habituales: por ejemplo, cuándo sueles ir a trabajar o a qué hora sueles comer.

⚙ **Lenguaje** Present simple
Aa Vocabulario Actividades diarias
🧩 **Habilidad** Hablar de tus actividades diarias

13.1 PUNTO CLAVE PRESENT SIMPLE

Para formar el present simple, utiliza la forma base del verbo (el infinitivo sin "to").

Forma base del verbo "to eat".

I eat lunch at noon every day.

She eats lunch at 2pm every day.

Si el sujeto es "he", "she" o "it", añade "s" a la forma base del verbo.

13.2 MÁS EJEMPLOS PRESENT SIMPLE

You get up at 7 o'clock.

We start work at 9 o'clock.

They leave work at 5pm.

She gets up at 5:30am.

He starts work at 11am.

Rob leaves work at 7pm.

13.3 CÓMO FUNCIONA PRESENT SIMPLE

Forma base del verbo.

SUJETO	VERBO	RESTO DE LA FRASE
I / You / We / They	eat	lunch at 2pm every day.
He / She / It	eats	

Si el sujeto es "he", "she" o "it", añade "s".

13.4 TACHA LA PALABRA INCORRECTA DE CADA FRASE

She ~~eat~~ / eats dinner in the evening.

1 He wake up / wakes up at 7 o'clock.

2 You leave / leaves home at 8:30am.

3 I start / starts work at 10am.

4 Ellen get / gets up at 5 o'clock.

5 My wife take / takes a shower in the evening.

6 I take / takes a shower in the morning.

7 My parents eat / eats lunch at 2pm.

8 We leave / leaves work at 4pm.

9 My brother work / works with animals.

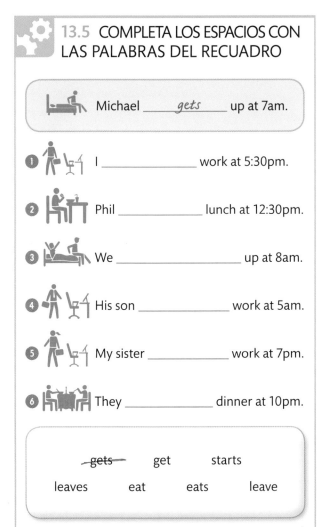

13.5 COMPLETA LOS ESPACIOS CON LAS PALABRAS DEL RECUADRO

Michael ___gets___ up at 7am.

1 I _____ work at 5:30pm.

2 Phil _____ lunch at 12:30pm.

3 We _____ up at 8am.

4 His son _____ work at 5am.

5 My sister _____ work at 7pm.

6 They _____ dinner at 10pm.

~~gets~~   get   starts

leaves   eat   eats   leave

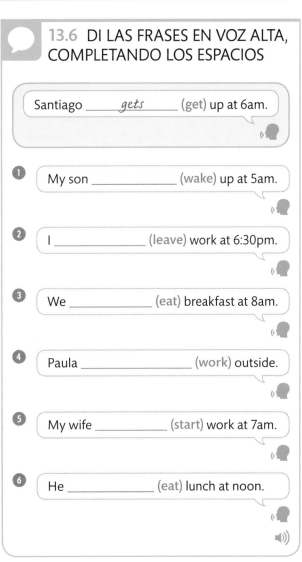

13.6 DI LAS FRASES EN VOZ ALTA, COMPLETANDO LOS ESPACIOS

Santiago ___gets___ (get) up at 6am.

1 My son _____ (wake) up at 5am.

2 I _____ (leave) work at 6:30pm.

3 We _____ (eat) breakfast at 8am.

4 Paula _____ (work) outside.

5 My wife _____ (start) work at 7am.

6 He _____ (eat) lunch at noon.

13.7 PUNTO CLAVE FINALES EN "S" Y "ES"

En los verbos terminados en "sh", "ch", "o", "ss", "x" y "z",
con "he", "she" o "it" añade "es".

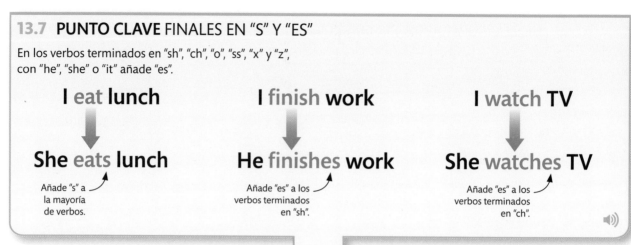

I eat lunch

She eats lunch

Añade "s" a
la mayoría
de verbos.

I finish work

He finishes work

Añade "es" a los
verbos terminados
en "sh".

I watch TV

She watches TV

Añade "es" a los
verbos terminados
en "ch".

13.8 PRONUNCIACIÓN PRONUNCIAR "S" Y "ES"

Las terminaciones en "s" se pronuncian
de manera diferente. Escucha la diferencia.

eats

Suena como
una "s".

leaves

Suena como
una "z".

watches

Pronuncia la partícula
"es" como el verbo "is".

13.9 DI LAS PALABRAS EN VOZ ALTA

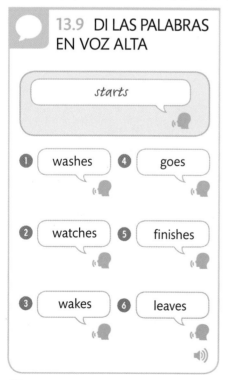

starts

1. washes
2. watches
3. wakes
4. goes
5. finishes
6. leaves

13.10 COMPLETA LOS ESPACIOS CON LA FORMA CORRECTA DEL VERBO

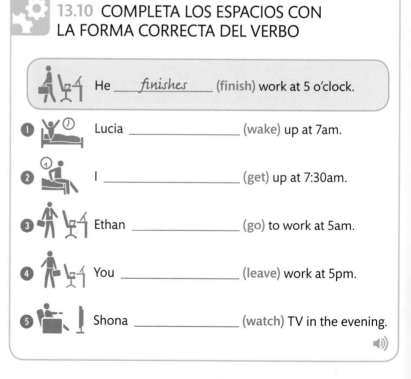

He ___*finishes*___ (finish) work at 5 o'clock.

1. Lucia _____ (wake) up at 7am.

2. I _____ (get) up at 7:30am.

3. Ethan _____ (go) to work at 5am.

4. You _____ (leave) work at 5pm.

5. Shona _____ (watch) TV in the evening.

13.11 VUELVE A ESCRIBIR LAS FRASES CORRIGIENDO LOS ERRORES

> Our children eats breakfast at 8am.
> _Our children eat breakfast at 8am._

1 My mother watchs TV in the morning.

_____

2 We goes to bed at midnight.

_____

3 My husband finishs work at 6:30pm.

_____

4 Rob go to work at 8:30am.

_____

5 I takes a shower in the morning.

_____

6 I leaves work at 6 o'clock in the evening.

_____

13.12 ESCUCHA EL AUDIO Y RESPONDE A LAS PREGUNTAS

Joan habla sobre su rutina diaria y su horario de trabajo.

> She starts work at 4pm.
> **True** ☐ **False** ☑

1 She finishes work at 12pm.
True ☐ **False** ☐

2 She eats lunch at 1pm.
True ☐ **False** ☐

3 She has dinner at 7:30pm.
True ☐ **False** ☐

4 She watches TV in the afternoon.
True ☐ **False** ☐

5 She goes on the computer in the evening.
True ☐ **False** ☐

6 She goes to bed at 8:30pm.
True ☐ **False** ☐

13.13 USA EL DIAGRAMA PARA CREAR 12 FRASES CORRECTAS Y DILAS EN VOZ ALTA

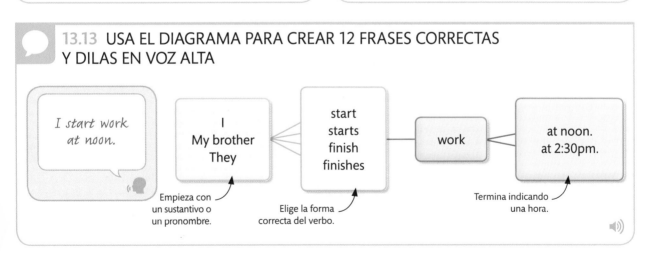

I start work at noon.

| I / My brother / They | start / starts / finish / finishes | work | at noon. / at 2:30pm. |

Empieza con un sustantivo o un pronombre.

Elige la forma correcta del verbo.

Termina indicando una hora.

14 Describir tu semana

Puedes hablar sobre lo que haces cada semana utilizando el presente y expresiones temporales. Estas, normalmente, se forman utilizando preposiciones y los días de la semana.

🔧 **Lenguaje** Días y preposiciones
Aa Vocabulario Días de la semana
🧩 **Habilidad** Hablar de tus rutinas semanales

14.1 VOCABULARIO DÍAS DE LA SEMANA

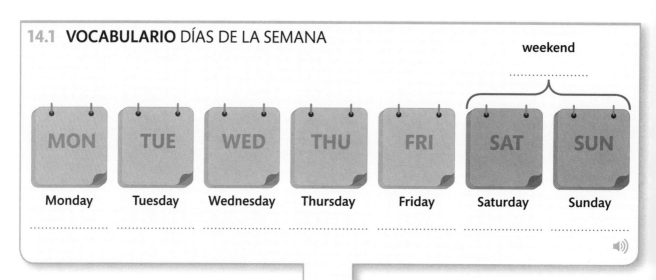

weekend

MON — Monday
TUE — Tuesday
WED — Wednesday
THU — Thursday
FRI — Friday
SAT — Saturday
SUN — Sunday

14.2 PUNTO CLAVE PREPOSICIONES Y DÍAS DE LA SEMANA

Utiliza "on" antes del día de la semana para concretar el día que haces algo.

Puedes añadir "-s" al día de la semana para indicar que algo se suele repetir siempre el mismo día de la semana.

I go to work on Mondays.

I work from Monday to Friday.

Utiliza "from" para indicar el día que empiezas a hacer algo.

Utiliza "to" para indicar el día que terminas de hacer algo.

NOTA
En inglés de Estados Unidos, puedes prescindir de "go to" y de la preposición cuando te refieras al día que trabajas: "I work Mondays".

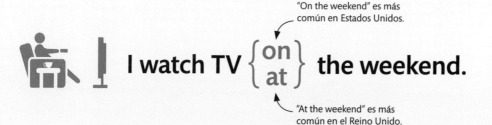

"On the weekend" es más común en Estados Unidos.

I watch TV { on / at } the weekend.

"At the weekend" es más común en el Reino Unido.

14.3 COMPLETA LOS ESPACIOS Y ACABA LAS FRASES

Sharon wakes up at 5am __*on*__ Mondays.

1 We eat lunch at 3pm _____ the weekend.

2 She goes to bed at 1am _____ the weekend.

3 I go to work _____ Monday _____ Wednesday.

4 They eat dinner at 9pm _____ the weekend.

5 We finish work at 3pm _____ Fridays.

6 I eat breakfast at work _____ Mondays.

14.4 **VOCABULARIO** ACTIVIDADES

go to the gym   go swimming   play tennis   play soccer   read the newspaper   take a bath

Aa 14.5 COMPLETA LOS ESPACIOS Y ACABA LAS FRASES

 She _*plays tennis*_ on Mondays.

1 He _____ on Tuesdays and Fridays.

2 They _____ on Thursdays.

3 He _____ on Wednesdays.

4 I _____ on the weekend.

5 You _____ on Saturdays.

14.6 DI LAS FRASES EN ALTO, COMPLETANDO LOS ESPACIOS

I play tennis __*on*__ Wednesdays.

1 I watch TV _____ Sundays.

2 I take a bath _____ 7pm every day.

3 I go to bed _____ 10 o'clock _____ Sundays.

4 I get up _____ 8am _____ Monday to Friday.

51

14.7 VOCABULARIO FRASES QUE INDICAN FRECUENCIA

Utiliza las expresiones que indican frecuencia para mostrar la periodicidad con que sucede algo.

once a week

twice a week

three times a week

every day

14.8 CÓMO FUNCIONA USAR FRASES QUE INDICAN FRECUENCIA

Normalmente, las frases que indican frecuencia suelen ir al final de la oración.

PRESENTE	FRECUENCIA
I go to the gym	**twice a week.**

14.9 MÁS EJEMPLOS FRASES QUE INDICAN FRECUENCIA

He goes to work three times a week.

She goes swimming four times a week.

We eat dinner at 7:30pm every day.

They watch TV five times a week.

14.10 ESCUCHA EL AUDIO Y MARCA LA RESPUESTA A LAS PREGUNTAS

Angela wakes up at 5:30am every day.
True ☐ **False** ☑

❶ Fred works from 8am to 6pm five times a week.
True ☐ **False** ☐

❷ Scott has dinner at 6am.
True ☐ **False** ☐

❸ Linda has a shower every morning.
True ☐ **False** ☐

❹ Jennifer watches TV on the weekend.
True ☐ **False** ☐

❺ Tim's daughter goes to bed at 7:30pm on Sundays.
True ☐ **False** ☐

14.11 ESCRIBE LAS FRASES EN EL ORDEN CORRECTO

every | day. | a shower | has | He

He has a shower every day.

① get up | five days | I | at 6am | a week.

② every | day. | They | at 11pm | go to bed

③ plays | soccer | Sarah | twice a week.

④ once | his clothes | a week. | washes | Jamie

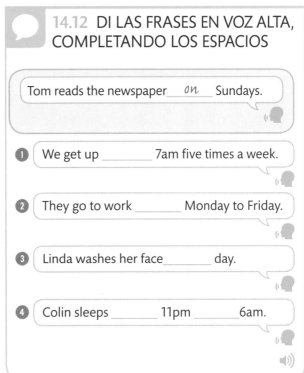

14.12 DI LAS FRASES EN VOZ ALTA, COMPLETANDO LOS ESPACIOS

Tom reads the newspaper _on_ Sundays.

① We get up _____ 7am five times a week.

② They go to work _____ Monday to Friday.

③ Linda washes her face _____ day.

④ Colin sleeps _____ 11pm _____ 6am.

---

14 ✓ CHECKLIST

⚙ Días y preposiciones ☐   **Aa** Días de la semana ☐   🧩 Hablar de tus rutinas semanales ☐

↻ REPASA LO QUE HAS APRENDIDO EN LAS UNIDADES 9–14

NUEVO LENGUAJE	FRASES DE EJEMPLO	☑	UNIDAD
HABLAR DE TU TRABAJO	I am **a police officer.** He is **an engineer.**	☐	10.1
USAR "WORK IN", "WORK ON" Y "WORK WITH"	I work in **a hospital.** I work on **a farm.** I work with **animals.**	☐	10.8, 10.11
DECIR LA HORA	It's **five.** It's **five o'clock.**	☐	11.1, 11.2
EL PRESENTE	I eat **lunch at noon every day.** She eats **lunch at 2pm every day.**	☐	13.1
DÍAS Y PREPOSICIONES	I work **on Mondays.** I work **from Monday to Friday.**	☐	14.2
FRASES QUE INDICAN FRECUENCIA	I go to the gym **twice a week.**	☐	14.8, 14.9

15 Frases negativas con "to be"

Para hacer una frase negativa se utiliza "not" o la forma contraída "n't". Las frases negativas con el verbo "to be" siguen reglas diferentes que las formadas con otros verbos.

⚙ **Lenguaje** Frases negativas con "to be"
Aa Vocabulario "Not"
🧩 **Habilidad** Decir lo que las cosas no son

15.1 PUNTO CLAVE FRASES NEGATIVAS CON EL VERBO "TO BE"

Añade "not" después del verbo "to be" para hacer la frase negativa.

I am **a farmer. I am not a doctor.**

Se añade "not" para hacer la frase negativa.

🔊

15.2 MÁS EJEMPLOS FRASES NEGATIVAS CON EL VERBO "TO BE"

 He is **not an adult.**

 It is **not 5 o'clock.**

 They are **not engineers.**

 This is **not a pig.**

 We are **not actors.**

 That is **not my bag.**

🔊

15.3 CÓMO FUNCIONA FRASES NEGATIVAS CON EL VERBO "TO BE"

La forma del verbo "to be" es la misma si la frase es negativa o positiva. La única diferencia es la inclusión de "not".

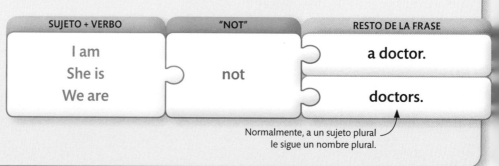

SUJETO + VERBO	"NOT"	RESTO DE LA FRASE
I am She is We are	not	a doctor. doctors.

Normalmente, a un sujeto plural le sigue un nombre plural.

15.4 VUELVE A ESCRIBIR LAS FRASES PONIENDO LAS PALABRAS EN EL ORDEN CORRECTO

gardener. | Jack | not | is | a

Jack is not a gardener.

1 sister. | my | She | not | is

_____

2 her | not | car. | is | That

_____

3 years | I | old. | not | am | 35

_____

4 are | not | Spanish. | We

_____

5 vet. | Chad | a | not | is

_____

15.5 COMPLETA LOS ESPACIOS PARA FORMAR FRASES NEGATIVAS

It _____*is not*_____ 11 o'clock.

1 He _____ in the office.

2 She _____ a businesswoman.

3 I _____ 18 years old.

4 This _____ a snake.

5 We _____ artists.

6 You _____ at work.

7 Dexter _____ a cat.

15.6 ESCUCHA EL AUDIO Y LUEGO NUMERA LAS IMÁGENES EN EL ORDEN EN QUE SE DESCRIBEN

A ☐

B 1

C ☐

D ☐

E ☐

15.7 PUNTO CLAVE FORMAS NEGATIVAS CORTAS

"You are not" se puede contraer de dos maneras diferentes. Se pueden contraer el sujeto y el verbo, o bien el verbo y la partícula "not".

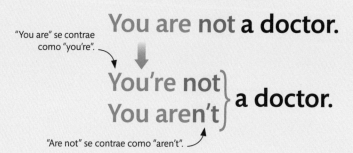

"You are" se contrae como "you're".

You are not a doctor.

↓

You're not
You aren't } **a doctor.**

"Are not" se contrae como "aren't".

15.8 MÁS EJEMPLOS FORMAS NEGATIVAS CORTAS

I am not a teacher.

↓

I'm not a teacher.

No puedes decir "I amn't."

He is not a farmer.

↓

He's not
He isn't } **a farmer.**

She is not American.

↓

She's not
She isn't } **American.**

It is not a pencil.

↓

It's not
It isn't } **a pencil.**

We are not waiters.

↓

We're not
We aren't } **waiters.**

They are not British.

↓

They're not
They aren't } **British.**

15.9 VUELVE A ESCRIBIR LAS FRASES CORRIGIENDO LOS ERRORES

Louis aren't Hayley's uncle.
Louis isn't Hayley's uncle.

❶ It am not 10 o'clock in the morning.

_____

❷ You isn't 35 years old.

_____

❸ I aren't Australian.

_____

❹ My brother aren't married.

_____

❺ Tom and Angela isn't construction workers.

_____

15.10 LEE EL BLOG Y RESPONDE A LAS PREGUNTAS

Françoise is 33 years old.
True ☐ **False** ☑

1 She isn't from the USA.
True ☐ **False** ☐

2 She speaks French.
True ☐ **False** ☐

3 She is French.
True ☐ **False** ☐

4 Her husband speaks English.
True ☐ **False** ☐

5 Her husband is British.
True ☐ **False** ☐

6 They live in the USA.
True ☐ **False** ☐

7 Her husband isn't a student.
True ☐ **False** ☐

My life Blog

HOME | ENTRIES | ABOUT | CONTACT

POSTED TUESDAY, OCTOBER 16

ABOUT ME

My name is Françoise, and I'm 35 years old. I speak French, but I'm not from France. I'm from Québec. I'm married to a man called Henry. He speaks English, but he isn't from North America and he isn't from Britain. He's from New Zealand. We don't live in Québec or New Zealand. We live in Ohio, USA. We are graduate students there.

15.11 USA EL DIAGRAMA PARA CREAR 12 FRASES CORRECTAS Y DILAS EN VOZ ALTA

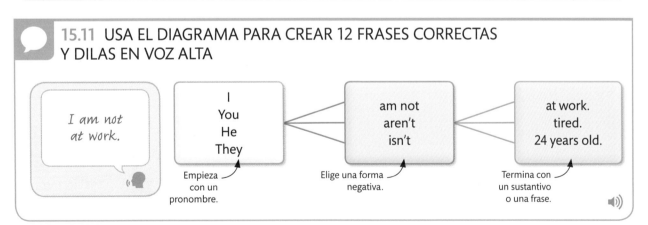

I am not at work.

| I You He They | am not aren't isn't | at work. tired. 24 years old. |

Empieza con un pronombre.

Elige una forma negativa.

Termina con un sustantivo o una frase.

15 ✓ **CHECKLIST**

⚙ Frases negativas con "to be" ☐   **Aa** "Not" ☐   🧩 Decir lo que las cosas no son ☐

16 Más frases negativas

Añade "do not" o "does not" antes de la mayoría de los verbos para hacer su forma negativa. Es habitual acortar estas formas escribiendo "don't" o "doesn't".

⚙ **Lenguaje** Present simple negativo
Aa Vocabulario Actividades diarias
🧩 **Habilidad** Decir lo que no haces

16.1 PUNTO CLAVE PRESENT SIMPLE NEGATIVO

Para construir la forma negativa con "I", "you", "we" o "they" añade "do not". Con "he", "she" o "it" añade "does not".

I work **outside**.

El verbo principal no cambia.

I do not work **outside**.
I work **inside**.

He works **inside**.

He does not work **inside**.
He works **outside**.

16.2 MÁS EJEMPLOS PRESENT SIMPLE NEGATIVO

 You do not have **a laptop**.

 We do not start **work at 8am**.

 He does not live **in Los Angeles**.

 The house does not have **a backyard**.

16.3 CÓMO FUNCIONA PRESENT SIMPLE NEGATIVO

Utiliza "do" o "does" con "not" seguido de la forma base del verbo principal (el infinitivo sin "to").

SUJETO	"DO / DOES" + "NOT"	FORMA BASE	RESTO DE LA FRASE
I / You / We / They	do not	work	outside.
He / She / It	does not		

16.4 COMPLETA LOS ESPACIOS CON "DO NOT" O "DOES NOT"

She _does not_ go to the gym on Thursdays.

1 I _____ read the papers on Saturday.

2 The dog _____ eat fish.

3 They _____ go to the theater often.

4 Ben and I _____ live on a farm now.

5 Theo _____ cycle to work.

6 You _____ work at Fabio's café.

7 Claire _____ watch TV in the evening.

8 We _____ play football at home.

9 Pierre _____ wake up before noon.

16.5 ESCUCHA EL AUDIO Y RESPONDE A LAS PREGUNTAS

Frank habla acerca de sus rutinas diaria y semanal.

Frank works in a store on Queen Street.
True ☑ **False** ☐

1 Frank gets up at 5am.
True ☐ **False** ☐

2 Frank has lunch at 1pm every day.
True ☐ **False** ☐

3 Frank goes swimming on Wednesday evening.
True ☐ **False** ☐

4 Frank watches TV every night before bed.
True ☐ **False** ☐

16.6 PUNTO CLAVE FORMAS NEGATIVAS CONTRAÍDAS

En inglés, "do not" y "does not" se contraen muy a menudo como "don't" y "doesn't".

I do not work **outside.**   He does not work **outside.**

I don't work **outside.**   He doesn't work **outside.**

16.7 MÁS EJEMPLOS PRESENT SIMPLE NEGATIVO: FORMAS CORTAS

 You don't play **soccer.**

 She doesn't speak **English.**

 We don't want **that cake.**

 He doesn't live **near here.**

16.8 COMPLETA LOS ESPACIOS Y ESCRIBE CADA FRASE DE TRES MANERAS DISTINTAS

I get up at 7am.	I do not get up at 7am.	I don't get up at 7am.
❶ _____	_____	We don't go to work every day.
❷ _____	He does not watch TV in the evening.	_____
❸ You work in an office.	_____	_____
❹ _____	_____	They don't play tennis.
❺ _____	She does not work with children.	_____

16.9 VUELVE A ESCRIBIR LAS FRASES CORRIGIENDO LOS ERRORES

He don't play soccer on Saturdays.
He doesn't play soccer on Saturdays.

❶ We doesn't work with animals.

_____

❷ I doesn't eat chocolate.

_____

❸ Sandy don't work in a hairdresser's.

_____

❹ Melanie and Cris doesn't have a car.

_____

❺ They doesn't live in Park Road now.

_____

❻ We doesn't watch Hollywood movies.

_____

❼ She don't drive a taxi.

_____

🔊

16.10 USA EL DIAGRAMA PARA CREAR 12 FRASES CORRECTAS Y DILAS EN VOZ ALTA

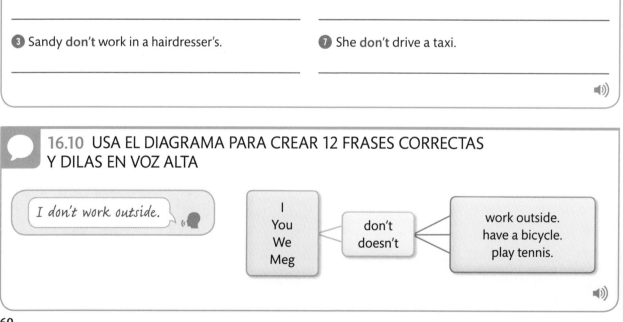

I don't work outside.

| I / You / We / Meg | don't / doesn't | work outside. / have a bicycle. / play tennis. |

🔊

16.11 LEE EL ARTÍCULO Y RESPONDE A LAS PREGUNTAS

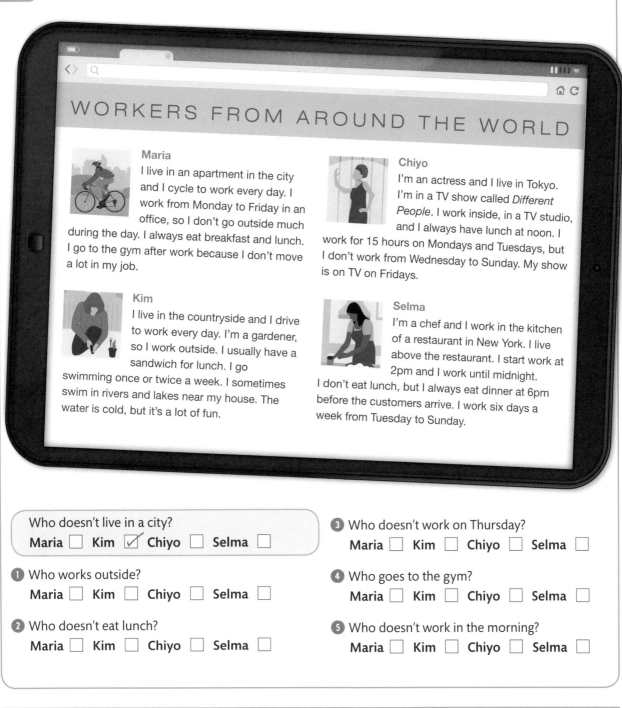

WORKERS FROM AROUND THE WORLD

Maria
I live in an apartment in the city and I cycle to work every day. I work from Monday to Friday in an office, so I don't go outside much during the day. I always eat breakfast and lunch. I go to the gym after work because I don't move a lot in my job.

Chiyo
I'm an actress and I live in Tokyo. I'm in a TV show called *Different People*. I work inside, in a TV studio, and I always have lunch at noon. I work for 15 hours on Mondays and Tuesdays, but I don't work from Wednesday to Sunday. My show is on TV on Fridays.

Kim
I live in the countryside and I drive to work every day. I'm a gardener, so I work outside. I usually have a sandwich for lunch. I go swimming once or twice a week. I sometimes swim in rivers and lakes near my house. The water is cold, but it's a lot of fun.

Selma
I'm a chef and I work in the kitchen of a restaurant in New York. I live above the restaurant. I start work at 2pm and I work until midnight. I don't eat lunch, but I always eat dinner at 6pm before the customers arrive. I work six days a week from Tuesday to Sunday.

Who doesn't live in a city?
Maria ☐ **Kim** ☐ **Chiyo** ☑ **Selma** ☐

❶ Who works outside?
Maria ☐ **Kim** ☐ **Chiyo** ☐ **Selma** ☐

❷ Who doesn't eat lunch?
Maria ☐ **Kim** ☐ **Chiyo** ☐ **Selma** ☐

❸ Who doesn't work on Thursday?
Maria ☐ **Kim** ☐ **Chiyo** ☐ **Selma** ☐

❹ Who goes to the gym?
Maria ☐ **Kim** ☐ **Chiyo** ☐ **Selma** ☐

❺ Who doesn't work in the morning?
Maria ☐ **Kim** ☐ **Chiyo** ☐ **Selma** ☐

16 ✔ CHECKLIST

⚙ Present simple negativo ☐ **Aa** Actividades diarias ☐ 🧩 Decir lo que no haces ☐

17 Preguntas simples

Para hacer preguntas simples con el verbo "to be", basta con cambiar el orden de sujeto y verbo. Normalmente, la respuesta a una pregunta simple empieza con "yes" o "no".

- ⚙ **Lenguaje** Preguntas simples
- **Aa Vocabulario** Trabajos y actividades habituales
- 🧩 **Habilidad** Hacer preguntas simples

17.1 PUNTO CLAVE PREGUNTAS CON "TO BE"

Para hacer una pregunta con el verbo "to be", pon el verbo antes del sujeto.

En una afirmación el sujeto siempre se coloca delante del verbo.

You are **Canadian.**

Are you **Canadian?**

En una pregunta, el verbo pasa al principio de la frase.

El sujeto se coloca después del verbo.

17.2 MÁS EJEMPLOS PREGUNTAS CON "TO BE"

Is Judi **an actor?**

Is he **French?**

Are they **engineers?**

Are you **a student?**

17.3 CÓMO FUNCIONA PREGUNTAS CON "TO BE"

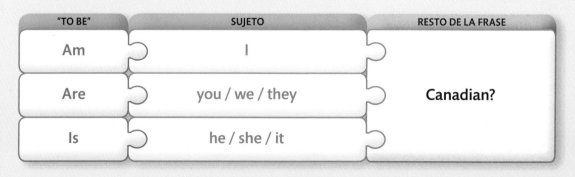

"TO BE"	SUJETO	RESTO DE LA FRASE
Am	I	
Are	you / we / they	Canadian?
Is	he / she / it	

17.4 VUELVE A ESCRIBIR LAS AFIRMACIONES COMO PREGUNTAS

She is a gardener.
Is she a gardener?

1 Brad is a nurse.

_____

2 These are my keys.

_____

3 Ruby and Farid are actors.

_____

4 This is his laptop.

_____

5 Valeria is his sister.

_____

🔊

17.5 ESCUCHA EL AUDIO E INDICA LA RESPUESTA CORRECTA A CADA PREGUNTA

17.6 ENTONACIÓN PREGUNTAS SIMPLES

El tono de voz suele subir al final de una pregunta simple en inglés.

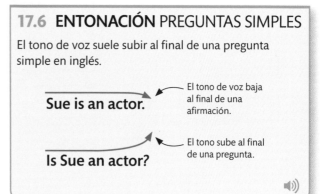

Sue is an actor. — El tono de voz baja al final de una afirmación.

Is Sue an actor? — El tono sube al final de una pregunta.

🔊

17.7 DI LAS FRASES EN VOZ ALTA, COMPLETANDO LOS ESPACIOS

Is _____ she a waitress?

1 _____ Holly your mother?

2 _____ they from Argentina?

3 _____ you a teacher?

4 _____ this your dog?

5 _____ there a post office?

🔊

17.8 PUNTO CLAVE PREGUNTAS CON "DO" Y "DOES"

Para hacer preguntas sin utilizar el verbo "to be", empiézalas con "do" o "does".

You work in an office.

↓

Do you work in an office?

Añade "do" a las preguntas cuyo sujeto sea "I", "you", "we" o "they".

She works in a school.

↓

Does she work in a school?

Si el sujeto es "he", "she" o "it", añade "does".

El verbo principal se escribe en su forma base (infinitivo sin "to")

🔊

17.9 MÁS EJEMPLOS PREGUNTAS CON "DO" Y "DOES"

 Do they live in Paris?

 Does Tom get up at 6am?

 Do you finish work at 4pm today?

 Does the party start at 7pm?

🔊

17.10 CÓMO FUNCIONA PREGUNTAS CON "DO" Y "DOES"

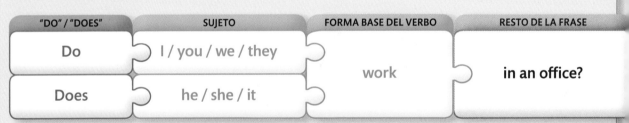

"DO" / "DOES"	SUJETO	FORMA BASE DEL VERBO	RESTO DE LA FRASE
Do	I / you / we / they	work	in an office?
Does	he / she / it		

17.11 COMPLETA LOS ESPACIOS EN LAS PREGUNTAS UTILIZANDO "DO" O "DOES"

Does she play tennis on Tuesdays?

❶ _____ you get up at 7am?

❷ _____ they live at number 59?

❸ _____ we finish work at 6pm today?

❹ _____ the parrot talk all day?

❺ _____ you work in a lab?

🔊

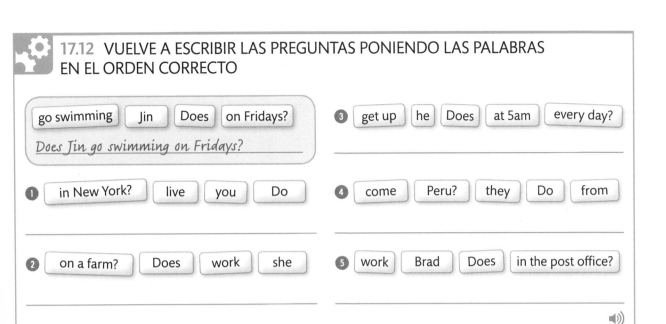

17.12 VUELVE A ESCRIBIR LAS PREGUNTAS PONIENDO LAS PALABRAS EN EL ORDEN CORRECTO

go swimming | Jin | Does | on Fridays?

Does Jin go swimming on Fridays?

❶ in New York? | live | you | Do

_____

❷ on a farm? | Does | work | she

_____

❸ get up | he | Does | at 5am | every day?

_____

❹ come | Peru? | they | Do | from

_____

❺ work | Brad | Does | in the post office?

_____

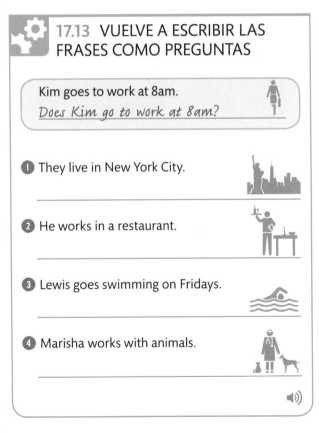

17.13 VUELVE A ESCRIBIR LAS FRASES COMO PREGUNTAS

Kim goes to work at 8am.
Does Kim go to work at 8am?

❶ They live in New York City.

_____

❷ He works in a restaurant.

_____

❸ Lewis goes swimming on Fridays.

_____

❹ Marisha works with animals.

_____

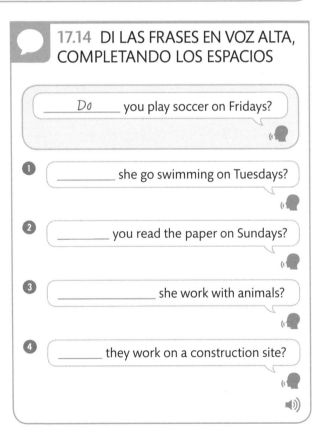

17.14 DI LAS FRASES EN VOZ ALTA, COMPLETANDO LOS ESPACIOS

___*Do*___ you play soccer on Fridays?

❶ _____ she go swimming on Tuesdays?

❷ _____ you read the paper on Sundays?

❸ _____ she work with animals?

❹ _____ they work on a construction site?

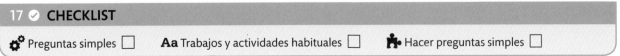

17 ✓ CHECKLIST

⚙ Preguntas simples ☐   **Aa** Trabajos y actividades habituales ☐   🧩 Hacer preguntas simples ☐

18 Responder preguntas

Cuando en inglés respondes a una pregunta, es habitual prescindir de palabras para acortar la respuesta. Las respuestas cortas se utilizan con frecuencia en el lenguaje hablado.

🔧 **Lenguaje** Respuestas cortas
Aa Vocabulario Trabajos y rutinas
🧩 **Habilidad** Responder preguntas orales

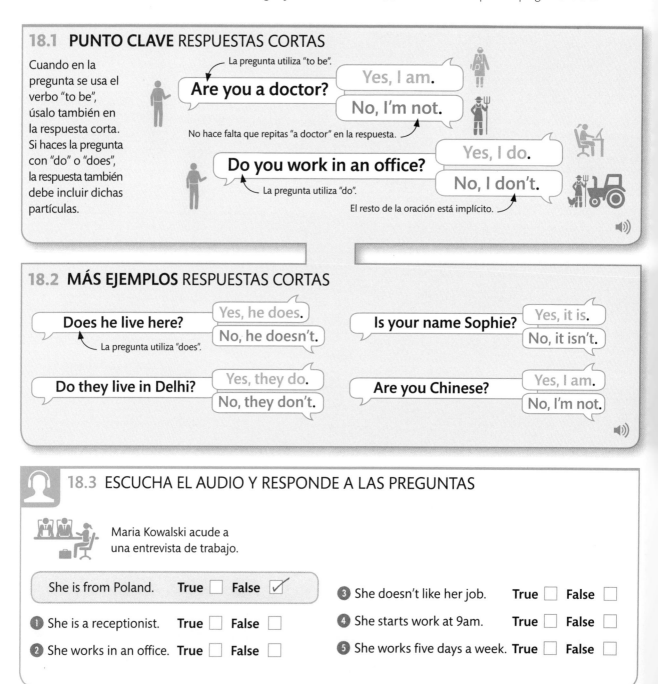

18.1 PUNTO CLAVE RESPUESTAS CORTAS

Cuando en la pregunta se usa el verbo "to be", úsalo también en la respuesta corta. Si haces la pregunta con "do" o "does", la respuesta también debe incluir dichas partículas.

La pregunta utiliza "to be".

Are you a doctor?

Yes, I am.

No, I'm not.

No hace falta que repitas "a doctor" en la respuesta.

Do you work in an office?

La pregunta utiliza "do".

Yes, I do.

No, I don't.

El resto de la oración está implícito.

18.2 MÁS EJEMPLOS RESPUESTAS CORTAS

Does he live here?

La pregunta utiliza "does".

Yes, he does.

No, he doesn't.

Is your name Sophie?

Yes, it is.

No, it isn't.

Do they live in Delhi?

Yes, they do.

No, they don't.

Are you Chinese?

Yes, I am.

No, I'm not.

18.3 ESCUCHA EL AUDIO Y RESPONDE A LAS PREGUNTAS

Maria Kowalski acude a una entrevista de trabajo.

She is from Poland. **True** ☐ **False** ✓

① She is a receptionist. **True** ☐ **False** ☐

② She works in an office. **True** ☐ **False** ☐

③ She doesn't like her job. **True** ☐ **False** ☐

④ She starts work at 9am. **True** ☐ **False** ☐

⑤ She works five days a week. **True** ☐ **False** ☐

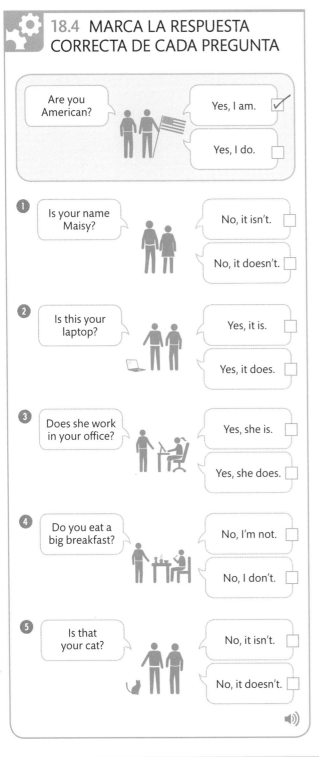

18.4 MARCA LA RESPUESTA CORRECTA DE CADA PREGUNTA

Are you American?
- Yes, I am. ✓
- Yes, I do.

1. Is your name Maisy?
   - No, it isn't.
   - No, it doesn't.

2. Is this your laptop?
   - Yes, it is.
   - Yes, it does.

3. Does she work in your office?
   - Yes, she is.
   - Yes, she does.

4. Do you eat a big breakfast?
   - No, I'm not.
   - No, I don't.

5. Is that your cat?
   - No, it isn't.
   - No, it doesn't.

18.5 RESPONDE A LAS PREGUNTAS EN VOZ ALTA

Does Joe watch TV?

Yes, _he does_.

1. Are you a student?

   No, _____.

2. Do they speak English?

   Yes, _____.

3. Is that your house?

   No, _____.

4. Does she play tennis?

   Yes, _____.

5. Is Miranda your aunt?

   No, _____.

6. Do they work in a hospital?

   Yes, _____.

7. Is he your grandfather?

   No, _____.

18 ✓ CHECKLIST

⚙ Respuestas cortas ☐   **Aa** Trabajos y rutinas ☐   🧩 Responder preguntas orales ☐

67

19 Hacer preguntas

Utiliza las palabras interrogativas "what", "who", "when" y "where" para hacer preguntas abiertas que no se pueden responder con "yes" o "no".

🔧 **Lenguaje** Preguntas abiertas
Aa Vocabulario Palabras interrogativas
🧩 **Habilidad** Preguntar sobre detalles

19.1 PUNTO CLAVE PREGUNTAS ABIERTAS CON EL VERBO "TO BE"

La palabra interrogativa se coloca al comienzo de la pregunta. Normalmente va seguida del verbo "to be".

> **My name is Sarah.**
> **What is your name?**

La palabra interrogativa se coloca al comienzo.

La pregunta es "abierta" porque no se puede responder con "yes" o "no".

19.2 MÁS EJEMPLOS PREGUNTAS ABIERTAS CON EL VERBO "TO BE"

What is Ruby's job?

What is the time?

What is in the bag?

What are we here for?

What is this thing?

What are Elliot's sisters called?

19.3 TACHA LAS PALABRAS INCORRECTAS DE CADA FRASE

What is / ~~are~~ / ~~am~~ the capital of France?

1 What is / are / am their names?

2 What is / are / am the time?

3 What is / are / am my favorite colors?

4 What is / are / am the hotel next to?

5 What is / are / am they?

6 What is / are / am your uncle's name?

7 What is / are / am my name?

19.4 VOCABULARIO
PALABRAS INTERROGATIVAS

Where

Who

When

Which

Why

How

19.5 MÁS EJEMPLOS PALABRAS INTERROGATIVAS

Where is the café?

Who is Jo's teacher?

When is dinner?

Which is your car?

Why am I here?

How are you?

Aa 19.6 CONECTA LAS PREGUNTAS CON SUS RESPUESTAS

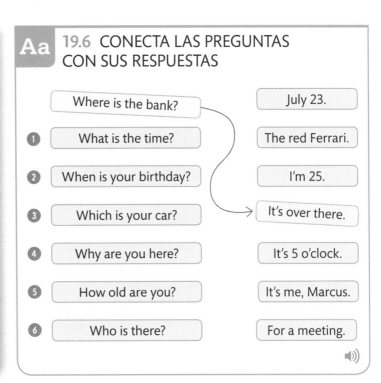

Where is the bank? — It's over there.

① What is the time? — It's 5 o'clock.

② When is your birthday? — July 23.

③ Which is your car? — The red Ferrari.

④ Why are you here? — For a meeting.

⑤ How old are you? — I'm 25.

⑥ Who is there? — It's me, Marcus.

19.7 COMPLETA LOS ESPACIOS CON LAS PALABRAS DEL RECUADRO

_____*What*_____ is your name?

① _____ are your parents from?

② _____ old are you?

③ _____ is breakfast?

④ _____ is your friend talking to?

⑤ _____ is it cold in here?

⑥ _____ person is your teacher?

What	Where	Who	When
Which		Why	How

69

19.8 PUNTO CLAVE PREGUNTAS ABIERTAS UTILIZANDO "DO" Y "DOES"

Para hacer una pregunta con la mayoría de verbos, utiliza la palabra interrogativa seguida por "do" o "does".

"Do" o "does" se coloca después de la palabra interrogativa.

When do you eat lunch?

La palabra interrogativa se coloca al principio.

El verbo principal cambia a su forma base.

19.9 CÓMO FUNCIONA PREGUNTAS ABIERTAS UTILIZANDO "DO" Y "DOES"

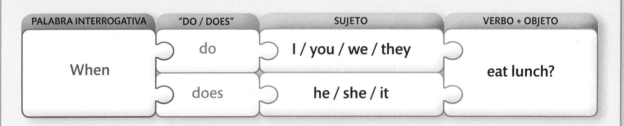

PALABRA INTERROGATIVA	"DO / DOES"	SUJETO	VERBO + OBJETO
When	do	I / you / we / they	eat lunch?
	does	he / she / it	

19.10 MÁS EJEMPLOS PREGUNTAS ABIERTAS UTILIZANDO "DO" Y "DOES"

Where do you go swimming?

When does he finish work?

What does she do on the weekend?

Which car do you drive to work?

19.11 COMPLETA LOS ESPACIOS Y ACABA LAS PREGUNTAS

When ___*do*___ they start work?

❶ When _____ she eat lunch?

❷ Where _____ they live?

❸ Which bag _____ you want?

❹ Where _____ he come from?

❺ When _____ the movie end?

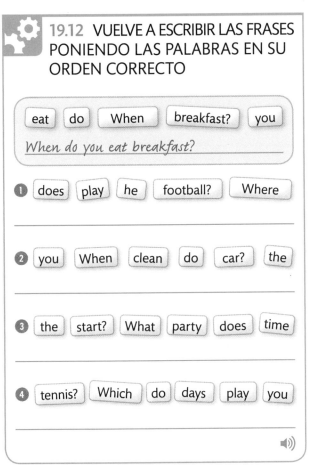

19.12 VUELVE A ESCRIBIR LAS FRASES PONIENDO LAS PALABRAS EN SU ORDEN CORRECTO

eat   do   When   breakfast?   you

When do you eat breakfast?

1 does   play   he   football?   Where

_____

2 you   When   clean   do   car?   the

_____

3 the   start?   What   party   does   time

_____

4 tennis?   Which   do   days   play   you

_____

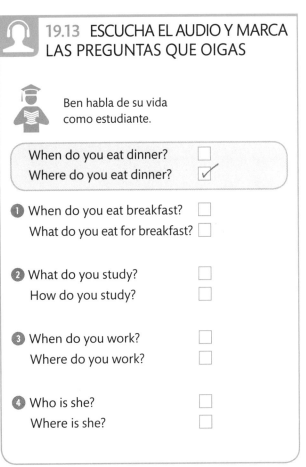

19.13 ESCUCHA EL AUDIO Y MARCA LAS PREGUNTAS QUE OIGAS

Ben habla de su vida como estudiante.

When do you eat dinner?   ☐
Where do you eat dinner?   ☑

1 When do you eat breakfast?   ☐
What do you eat for breakfast?   ☐

2 What do you study?   ☐
How do you study?   ☐

3 When do you work?   ☐
Where do you work?   ☐

4 Who is she?   ☐
Where is she?   ☐

19.14 DI LAS PREGUNTAS EN VOZ ALTA, COMPLETANDO LOS ESPACIOS CON LAS PALABRAS DEL RECUADRO

_____*What*_____ do you do for a living?

1 _____ do you work in the city?

2 _____ do you start work?

3 _____ time does it open?

4 _____ many people do you work with?

5 _____ do you work with?

| When | How | ~~What~~ | What | Where | Who |

19.15 LEE EL CORREO Y RESPONDE A LAS PREGUNTAS

Which village is Bernadette in?
Torremolinos ☐
Mijas ☑

1 Who is Bernadette on vacation with?
Her brother ☐
Her sister ☐

2 How many swimming pools does the hotel have?
Two ☐
Three ☐

3 What time does Bernadette get up?
At 7am ☐
At 7:30am ☐

4 What does Bernadette do in the morning?
Goes to the gym ☐
Goes swimming ☐

5 Where does Bernadette have breakfast?
In her room ☐
By the pool ☐

6 When is the flamenco dancing?
Tonight ☐
Tomorrow ☐

✉

To: Mary Jones

Subject: Vacation in Spain

Hi Mary.

We're in Spain, in a village called Mijas, near Torremolinos. My sister is at work this week, so I'm here with my brother, John. Our hotel is next to some apartments. It's in a complex and has two swimming pools and a gym. Breakfast is from 7:30am until 9 every morning, so I get up at 7am and have a swim before I eat. John stays in his room and we meet later for breakfast. The restaurant is by the pool. We have our breakfast there every day. There's also dancing at night. There's salsa dancing tonight, and tomorrow it's flamenco.

See you soon,
Bernadette

19.16 USA EL DIAGRAMA PARA CREAR 12 FRASES CORRECTAS Y DILAS EN VOZ ALTA

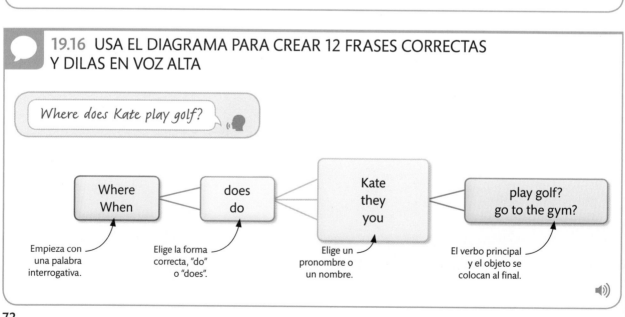

Where does Kate play golf?

| Where / When | does / do | Kate / they / you | play golf? / go to the gym? |

Empieza con una palabra interrogativa.

Elige la forma correcta, "do" o "does".

Elige un pronombre o un nombre.

El verbo principal y el objeto se colocan al final.

Where are my laptop?
Where is my laptop?

❶ How often does they play tennis?
_____

❷ Which office do he work in?
_____

❸ Where are the party?
_____

❹ What does you do?
_____

🔊

When _does Russell go to the gym?_
Russell goes to the gym on Tuesdays.

❶ What _____ ?
Her cat is called Ginger.

❷ Who _____ ?
My English teacher is Mrs. Price.

❸ Where _____ ?
Ben works in a hospital.

❹ How _____ ?
My grandmother is fine, thanks.

🔊

---

19 ✓ CHECKLIST

⚙ Preguntas abiertas ☐   **Aa** Palabras interrogativas ☐   🧩 Preguntar sobre detalles ☐

↻ REPASA LO QUE HAS APRENDIDO EN LAS UNIDADES 15–19

NUEVO LENGUAJE	FRASES DE EJEMPLO	☑	UNIDAD
FRASES NEGATIVAS CON "TO BE"	I am a farmer. I am not a doctor. You're not a doctor. You aren't a doctor.	☐	15.1, 15.3, 15.7
PRESENT SIMPLE NEGATIVO	He does not work inside. He works outside. I work outside. I do not work inside.	☐	16.1, 16.3, 16.6
PREGUNTAS SIMPLES	Are you Canadian? Do you work in an office? Does she work in a school?	☐	17.1, 17.8
RESPUESTAS CORTAS	Are you a doctor? Yes, I am. Do you work in an office? No, I don't.	☐	18.1, 18.2
PREGUNTAS ABIERTAS CON "TO BE"	My name is Sarah. What is your name?	☐	19.1, 19.2
PREGUNTAS ABIERTAS UTILIZANDO "DO" Y "DOES"	When do you eat lunch? When does she eat lunch?	☐	19.8, 19.9

20 Vocabulario

20.1 LA CIUDAD

village

town

city

hospital

police station

bus station

bus stop

train station

airport

school

factory

supermarket

store (US)
shop (UK)

pharmacy

bank

post office

library

museum

74

town hall

castle

office building

park

here

bridge

swimming pool

restaurant

café

there

bar

**movie theater (US)
cinema (UK)**

**theater (US)
theatre (UK)**

hotel

near

church

mosque

synagogue

temple

far

21 Hablar sobre tu ciudad

Cuando hablas sobre objetos, puedes utilizar "there is" para uno solo y "there are" para más de uno. "There isn't" y "there aren't" son las respectivas formas negativas.

⚙ **Lenguaje** "There is" y "there are"
Aa Vocabulario Ciudades y edificios
🧩 **Habilidad** Describir una ciudad

21.1 PUNTO CLAVE "THERE IS" Y "THERE ARE"

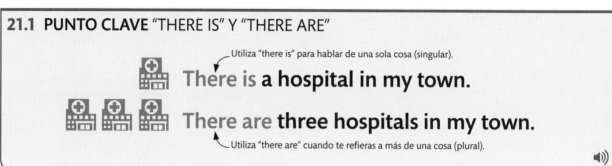

Utiliza "there is" para hablar de una sola cosa (singular).

There is a hospital in my town.

There are three hospitals in my town.

Utiliza "there are" cuando te refieras a más de una cosa (plural).

21.2 MÁS EJEMPLOS "THERE IS" Y "THERE ARE"

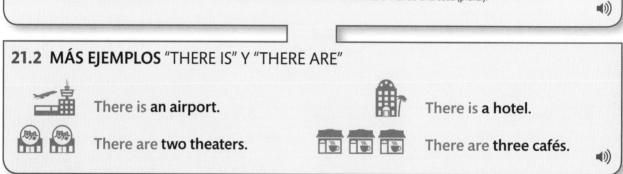

There is **an airport.**

There are **two theaters.**

There is **a hotel.**

There are **three cafés.**

21.3 COMPLETA LOS ESPACIOS CON "THERE IS" Y "THERE ARE"

_____There is_____ a factory.

1. _____ two churches.

2. _____ a swimming pool.

3. _____ a library.

4. _____ two castles.

21.4 DI ESTOS PLURALES EN VOZ ALTA

libraries

1. airports
2. theaters
3. schools
4. hospitals
5. bars
6. churches
7. factories
8. offices

Aa 21.5 OBSERVA LOS DIBUJOS Y COMPLETA LOS ESPACIOS PARA ACABAR LAS FRASES

There is a _town hall_ .

❶ There are _____ .

❷ There are _____ .

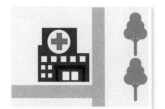

❸ There is a _____ .

❹ There is a _____ .

❺ There are _____ .

🔊

21.6 PUNTO CLAVE "THERE IS NOT" Y "THERE ARE NOT ANY"

Añade "not" para construir una frase negativa.

There is **not a school.**

There isn't **a school.**

Puedes contraer "is not" como "isn't".

Añade "not any" para construir una frase negativa en plural.

There are **not any schools.**

There aren't **any schools.**

Puedes contraer "are not" como "aren't".

🔊

21.7 TACHA LA PALABRA INCORRECTA DE CADA FRASE

There isn't / ~~aren't~~ a castle.

❶ There isn't / aren't a theater.

❷ There isn't / aren't any factories.

❸ There isn't / aren't a bus station.

❹ There isn't / aren't any airports.

❺ There isn't / aren't any churches.

🔊

21.8 OTRAS FORMAS "THERE AREN'T ANY"

Puedes utilizar "are no" en lugar de "aren't any". Significa lo mismo.

Esta es la forma contraída de "are not".

There aren't any **stores.**

There are no **stores.**

21.9 MÁS EJEMPLOS "ARE NO"

There are no **libraries in Oldtown.**

There are no **factories in Newport.**

There are no **schools in our village.**

21.10 COMPLETA LOS ESPACIOS UTILIZANDO "ARE" Y "AREN'T"

There _____*aren't*_____ any theaters.

❶ There _____ no castles.

❷ There _____ any factories.

❸ There _____ no hospitals.

❹ There _____ any churches.

❺ There _____ no swimming pools.

❻ There _____ no airports.

21.11 ESCUCHA EL AUDIO Y NUMERA LAS IMÁGENES EN EL ORDEN EN QUE SE DESCRIBEN

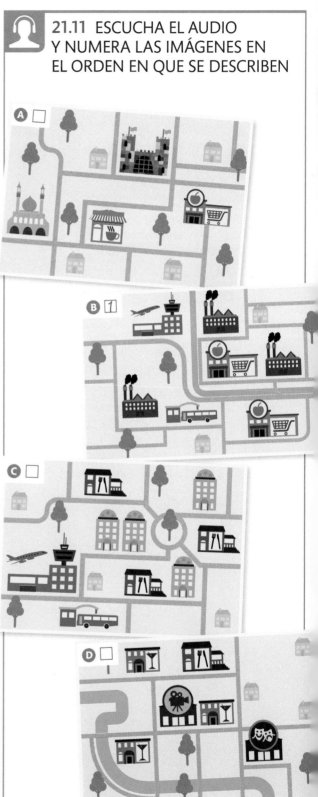

Ⓐ ☐

Ⓑ 1

Ⓒ ☐

Ⓓ ☐

21.12 LEE EL CORREO Y RESPONDE A LAS PREGUNTAS

There are two schools.
True ☐ **False** ☑

❶ There is a supermarket.
True ☐ **False** ☐

❷ There is a theater.
True ☐ **False** ☐

❸ There are four movie theaters.
True ☐ **False** ☐

❹ There are three restaurants.
True ☐ **False** ☐

✉ ⌄ ✕

To: Matt

Subject: Our new place

Hi Matt,

We're in our new house in Littleton and it's great! There are three schools in the town, so that's good for the children. There's also a big swimming pool and Joanne goes there every evening. I work in an office above the supermarket. It's near our house.

There are lots of things to do on the weekend. There isn't a theater, but there are two movie theaters, three restaurants, and a library. There's also a great museum. We go there every weekend because the children love it!

Come and see us soon. It's easy to get here. There isn't an airport or a train station, but there's a bus station.

See you soon! Jamal

↩ ↩↩   📎 🗑

21.13 OBSERVA EL DIBUJO Y DI LAS FRASES EN VOZ ALTA, COMPLETANDO LOS ESPACIOS

There is a supermarket. 🗣

❶ _____ a park. 🗣

❷ _____ a hotel. 🗣

❸ _____ no cafés. 🗣

❹ _____ an airport. 🗣

❺ _____ stores. 🗣

❻ _____ a train station. 🗣

❼ _____ theaters. 🗣

🔊

21 ✓ **CHECKLIST**

⚙ "There is" y "there are" ☐   **Aa** Ciudades y edificios ☐   🧩 Describir una ciudad ☐

22 Utilizar "a" y "the"

Utiliza el artículo definido ("the") o el artículo indefinido ("a", "an") para hablar de cosas de manera específica o general. Utiliza "some" para hablar de más de una cosa.

🛠 **Lenguaje** Artículos definidos e indefinidos
Aa Vocabulario Lugares en la ciudad
🧩 **Habilidad** Utilizar los artículos

22.1 PUNTO CLAVE "A / AN / THE"

Utiliza "a" para hablar de una cosa en general. Utiliza "the" para hablar de un lugar, persona o cosa que tú y tu interlocutor conocéis.

Utiliza "a" porque hablas de tu trabajo en general, no del lugar concreto donde trabajas.

I work in a library.

I work in the library on Main Street.

Utiliza "the" porque hablas del edificio en el que trabajas.

🔊

22.2 MÁS EJEMPLOS "A / AN / THE"

Utiliza "a/an" para hablar sobre los trabajos.

 Jim is an artist.

Utiliza "an" delante de palabras que comienzan con una vocal.

 Is there a bank near here?

Utiliza "a" con "is there" y "there is".

Utiliza "the" para hablar de un doctor en concreto.

 The doctor at my hospital is good.

 I go to the bank on Broad Street.

Utiliza "the" para hablar de un banco en concreto.

🔊

⚙ 22.3 TACHA LAS PALABRAS INCORRECTAS DE CADA FRASE

Charlotte is ~~a~~ / ~~an~~ / the actress.

1 A / An / **The** new teacher is called Miss Jones.

2 There is a / **an** / the good café in the park.

3 I work at a / an / **the** hotel next to the library.

4 There is **a** / an / the swimming pool near my office.

5 It is a / an / **the** dog's favorite toy.

6 Janie is a / **an** / the artist at the gallery.

7 See you at a / an / **the** café at the bus station.

🔊

22.4 PUNTO CLAVE "A / SOME"

"A" y "an" solo se pueden utilizar para nombres en singular. Para los plurales utiliza "some".

Utiliza "a" y "an" para hablar de una sola cosa.

Singular.

There is a hotel in the town.

Utiliza "some" para hablar de más de una cosa.

Plural.

There are some hotels in the town.

22.5 MÁS EJEMPLOS "A / SOME"

There is a bank on Main Street.

There are some banks on Main Street.

There is a waiter over there.

There are some children in the park.

22.6 COMPLETA LOS ESPACIOS CON "A" O "SOME"

There is ____*a*____ restaurant in the park.

1 There are _____ stores on Broad Street.

2 There is _____ café next to the castle.

3 There are _____ cakes on the table.

4 There is _____ phone here.

5 There are _____ factories downtown.

22.7 VUELVE A ESCRIBIR LAS FRASES CORRIGIENDO LOS ERRORES

There are a movie theater on Main Street.
There is a movie theater on Main Street.

1 There is some supermarkets in town.

_____

2 There are an office near the river.

_____

3 There is some chocolate bars in my bag.

_____

4 There are a hospital near the bus station.

_____

22.8 PUNTO CLAVE PREGUNTAS CON "A / ANY"

There is a hotel in the town.

Is there a hotel in the town?

Utiliza "a" para averiguar si
hay una unidad de algo.

There are some hotels in the town.

Are there any hotels in the town?

Utiliza "any" para averiguar si hay
una unidad de algo o más de una.

22.9 MÁS EJEMPLOS PREGUNTAS CON "A / ANY"

Is there a restaurant?

Is there a hospital?

Are there any factories?

Are there any theaters?

22.10 TACHA LAS PALABRAS INCORRECTAS EN CADA PREGUNTA

Is there a / ~~an~~ / ~~any~~ hospital in the town?

① Are there a / an / **any** stores on your street?

② Is there a / **an** / any airport near Littleton?

③ Are there a / an / **any** mosques in the city?

④ Is there **a** / an / any swimming pool downtown?

⑤ Are there a / an / **any** offices in that building?

22.11 VUELVE A ESCRIBIR LAS FRASES PONIENDO LAS PALABRAS EN SU ORDEN CORRECTO

| any | in | town? | Are | your | factories | there |

Are there any factories in your town?

① | there | here? | a | Is | supermarket | near |

_____

② | on | there | any | Elm Road? | Are | cafés |

_____

③ | Are | your house? | there | any | near | hotels |

_____

④ | a | café | office? | there | near | Is | your |

_____

⑤ | the | there | a bar | next to | Is | bank? |

_____

22.12 PUNTO CLAVE RESPUESTAS CORTAS

En inglés, cuando respondemos a una pregunta, no hace falta repetir todas las palabras de la pregunta.

Forma corta de: "Sí, hay un hotel en la ciudad".

Is there a hotel in the town?

Yes, there is.

No, there isn't.

Are there any hotels in the town?

Yes, there are.

No, there aren't.

Forma corta de: "No, no hay hoteles en la ciudad".

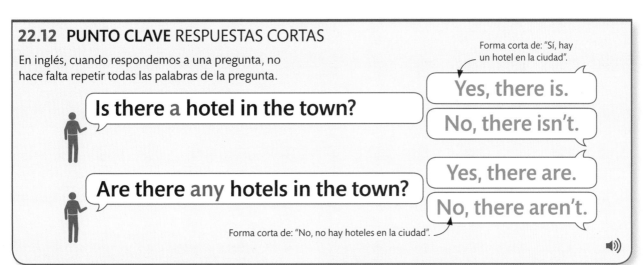

22.13 COMPLETA LOS ESPACIOS CON RESPUESTAS CORTAS

Are there any theaters in Littleton?
No, _there aren't_____.

① Is there a church on Main Street?
Yes, _____.

② Are there any pens in your bag?
Yes, _____.

③ Is there a post office near here?
No, _____.

④ Are there any supermarkets on Station Road?
Yes, _____.

⑤ Is there a school near your house?
No, _____.

⑥ Are there any dogs in the hotel?
No, _____.

22.14 OBSERVA EL MAPA Y RESPONDE A LAS PREGUNTAS EN VOZ ALTA

Is there a library?   _Yes, there is._

① Are there any hotels?   [   ]

② Is there a church?   [   ]

③ Are there two cafés?   [   ]

④ Is there a supermarket?   [   ]

23 Órdenes y direcciones

Utiliza el imperativo para decirle a alguien que haga algo. También se usa para hacer una advertencia, o para indicar una dirección a alguien.

⚙ **Lenguaje** Imperativo
Aa Vocabulario Direcciones
🧩 **Habilidad** Orientarse

23.1 PUNTO CLAVE IMPERATIVO

El imperativo se forma utilizando la forma base del verbo (el infinitivo sin "to").

Stop!

Forma base del verbo (el verbo es "to stop").

23.2 MÁS EJEMPLOS IMPERATIVO

Get **up.**

Be careful!

Eat **your breakfast.**

Help!

Give **that to me.**

Read **this book.**

23.3 ESCRIBE LOS IMPERATIVOS DE CADA INFINITIVO

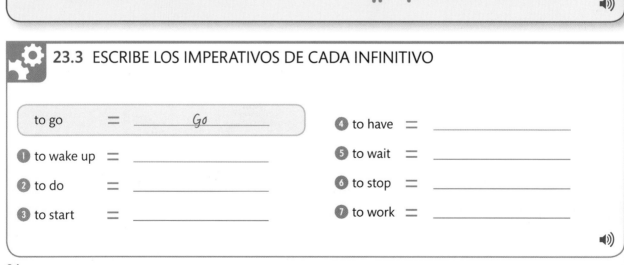

| to go | = | *Go* |

❶ to wake up =

❷ to do =

❸ to start =

❹ to have =

❺ to wait =

❻ to stop =

❼ to work =

23.4 PUNTO CLAVE
INDICAR DIRECCIONES

↑

go straight ahead

....

↰

turn left

....

↱

turn right

....

↑ 🏠

go past

....

take the first right

....

take the second right

....

🔊

23.5 MARCA LAS DIRECCIONES QUE TE LLEVARÁN EN EL MAPA A LOS LUGARES INDICADOS

You are here

For the Bridge Café:
Take the first right. The café is on the left. ☑
Take the first left. The café is on the right. ☐

❶ For the train station:
Take the second left. The station is on the right. ☐
Take the second right. The station is on the left. ☐

❷ For the Elm Tree Restaurant:
Take the first left, then turn right. The restaurant is on the right. ☐
Take the second left, then turn right. The restaurant is on the left. ☐

❸ For the hospital:
Take the second right, and the hospital is on the left. ☐
Take the second left, and the hospital is on the right. ☐

❹ For the Supreme Hotel:
Take the first left, then go straight ahead. The hotel is on the right. ☐
Take the first right, then go straight ahead. The hotel is on the left. ☐

❺ For the castle:
Take the first left, then turn right. The castle is on the left. ☐
Take the first left, then turn left. The castle is on the right. ☐

🔊

23.6 VOCABULARIO DIRECCIONES

next to

opposite

between

on the corner

behind

in front of

on the right

on the left

**intersection (US)
crossroads (UK)**

block

Aa 23.7 COMPLETA LOS ESPACIOS UTILIZANDO DIRECCIONES

The Rathbone Theater is
_____*opposite*_____ the park.

❶ The supermarket is

_____ the post office.

❷ The museum is

_____ the café.

❸ The station is

_____ the church.

❹ The cinema is on the

_____ of the intersection.

❺ The post office is_____

the café and the supermarket.

23.8 PUNTO CLAVE IMPERATIVO NEGATIVO

Añade "don't" o "do not" antes del verbo para construir el imperativo negativo.

Do not }
Don't } turn right.

23.9 MÁS EJEMPLOS IMPERATIVO NEGATIVO

Don't eat **that cake.**

Don't sit **there.**

 23.10 REESCRIBE LAS FRASES COMO IMPERATIVOS NEGATIVOS

Take the first left.
Don't take the first left.

❶ Read that book.

_____

❷ Go past the hotel.

_____

❸ Give that to the cat.

_____

❹ Have a shower.

_____

❺ Drive to the mall.

_____

23.11 ESCUCHA Y CONECTA LAS DIRECCIONES CON LOS LUGARES

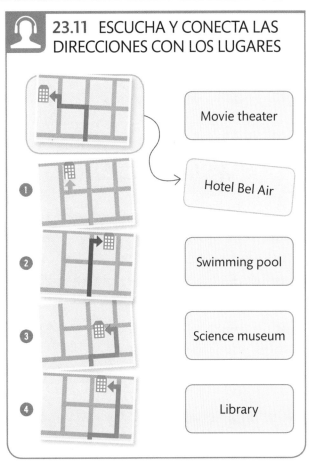

Movie theater

Hotel Bel Air

Swimming pool

Science museum

Library

---

24 Unir frases

"And" y "but" son conjunciones: palabras que unen frases.
"And" añade elementos a una frase o une varias en una sola.
"But" introduce un contraste en una frase.

⚙ **Lenguaje** Utilizar "and" y "but"
Aa Vocabulario Ciudad, trabajos y familia
🧩 **Habilidad** Unir frases

24.1 PUNTO CLAVE UTILIZAR "AND" PARA UNIR FRASES

Utiliza "and" para unir dos frases.

"There's" es lo mismo que "There is".

There's a library. There's a restaurant.

There's a library and a restaurant.

Cuando unes dos frases con "and" puedes prescindir del segundo "there's".

🔊

24.2 MÁS EJEMPLOS UTILIZAR "AND" PARA UNIR FRASES

Jazmin's sister lives and works in Paris.

My father and brother are both engineers.

Simon plays video games and watches TV every night.

🔊

24.3 UTILIZA "AND" PARA ESCRIBIR UNA ÚNICA FRASE CON LAS DOS AFIRMACIONES PROPUESTAS

I get up. I have a shower.
I get up and have a shower.

❶ There are two hotels. There are three shops.

_____

❷ Hilda works in a school. She works in a theater.

_____

❸ My uncle is a scientist. My aunt is a doctor.

_____

❹ Sue watches TV. She reads books.

_____

❺ The store opens at night. Jan starts work.

_____

🔊

24.4 ESCUCHA EL AUDIO Y CONECTA LOS LUGARES MENCIONADOS EN CADA AFIRMACIÓN CON "AND"

24.5 PUNTO CLAVE USAR UNA COMA EN LUGAR DE "AND"

Para listas de más de dos objetos, puedes utilizar comas en lugar de "and".

En una lista, puedes utilizar una coma en lugar de "and".

Utiliza otra coma antes de "and".

There's a library, a store, and a café.

Mantén "and" entre los dos sustantivos al final de la frase.

24.6 MARCA LAS FRASES QUE UTILIZAN LAS COMAS Y "AND" DE MANERA CORRECTA

I am a wife, a mother, and a daughter. ☑
I am a wife, and a mother, a daughter. ☐

❹ Teo plays with his car and his train and his bus. ☐
Teo plays with his car, train, and bus. ☐

❶ There are hotels and bars and stores. ☐
There are hotels, bars, and stores. ☐

❺ There is a pencil, a bag and, a cell phone. ☐
There is a pencil, a bag, and a cell phone. ☐

❷ Sam eats, breakfast lunch and dinner. ☐
Sam eats breakfast, lunch, and dinner. ☐

❻ My friends, girlfriend, and aunt are here. ☐
My friends, and, girlfriend and aunt are here. ☐

❸ I play tennis, soccer, and chess. ☐
I play tennis, and soccer, and chess. ☐

❼ Ling works on Monday, Thursday, and Friday. ☐
Ling works on Monday, and Thursday, Friday. ☐

24.7 PUNTO CLAVE UTILIZAR "BUT" PARA UNIR FRASES

Utiliza "but" para unir una afirmación positiva con otra negativa.

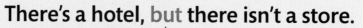

There's a hotel. There isn't a store.

⬇

There's a hotel, but there isn't a store.

Puedes utilizar "but" para añadir algo negativo a una frase positiva.

There isn't a store here, but there is a hotel.

Puedes utilizar "but" para añadir algo positivo a una frase negativa.

24.8 CONECTA EL COMIENZO Y EL FINAL DE CADA FRASE

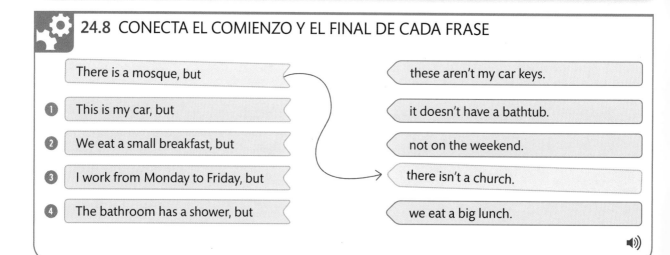

There is a mosque, but — there isn't a church.

① This is my car, but — these aren't my car keys.

② We eat a small breakfast, but — it doesn't have a bathtub.

③ I work from Monday to Friday, but — not on the weekend.

④ The bathroom has a shower, but — we eat a big lunch.

24.9 ESCRIBE UNA ÚNICA FRASE CON LAS DOS AFIRMACIONES PROPUESTAS

There is a post office. There isn't a bank.
There is a post office, but there isn't a bank.

① There isn't a bathtub. There is a shower.
_____

② There isn't a bar. There is a café.
_____

③ This bag is Maya's. That laptop isn't hers.
_____

④ Si doesn't have any dogs. He has two cats.
_____

⑤ Sally reads books. She never watches TV.
_____

24.10 TACHA LA PALABRA INCORRECTA DE CADA FRASE

I am a father and / ~~but~~ a son.

1. Lu reads books and / but magazines.

2. I work every weekday, and / but not on weekends.

3. Jim is a husband and / but a father.

4. There is a cinema, and / but no theater.

5. There isn't a gym, and / but there is a pool.

🔊

24.11 OBSERVA LA TABLA Y DI EN VOZ ALTA FRASES QUE INCLUYAN "AND" Y "BUT"

There is ___a mosque and a church, but there isn't a factory___.

1. There is _____.

2. There is _____.

3. There is _____.

4. There is _____.

🔊

24 ✅ CHECKLIST

⚙️ Utilizar "and" y "but" ☐   **Aa** Ciudad, trabajos y familia ☐   🧩 Unir frases ☐

25 Describir lugares

Utiliza los adjetivos para dar más información sobre los sustantivos, por ejemplo, para describir una persona, edificio o lugar.

⚙ **Lenguaje** Adjetivos
Aa Vocabulario Adjetivos y nombres de lugares
🧩 **Habilidad** Describir lugares

25.1 PUNTO CLAVE UTILIZAR ADJETIVOS

Los adjetivos se colocan normalmente antes del sustantivo que describen.

She is a busy woman.

He is a busy man.

Los adjetivos no tienen género y se utilizan por igual delante de un nombre masculino o femenino.

It is a busy town.

These are busy streets.

Los adjetivos no tienen número y se utilizan por igual delante de un nombre singular o plural.

🔊

25.2 VOCABULARIO ADJETIVOS

old
....

new
....

beautiful
....

horrible
....

busy
....

quiet
....

small
....

big
....

 🔊

25.3 VUELVE A ESCRIBIR LAS FRASES PONIENDO LAS PALABRAS EN SU ORDEN CORRECTO

a | This | is | town. | beautiful

This is a beautiful town.

1. horrible | is | He | man. | a

_____

2. are | They | small | children.

_____

3. uncle | My | man. | is | a quiet

_____

4. large | is | There | a | cake.

_____

5. my | shoes. | are | old | These

_____

6. supermarket. | a | new | is | There

_____

7. in | work | You | museum. | an old

_____

25.4 OTRAS FORMAS ADJETIVOS

A veces, los adjetivos pueden colocarse en distintos lugares dentro de la frase.

The town is busy.

Puedes poner el adjetivo al final de la frase, después del verbo "to be".

Southbay is a busy town.

Normalmente, el adjetivo se coloca antes del sustantivo.

It is busy.

Puedes reemplazar el sustantivo con un pronombre.

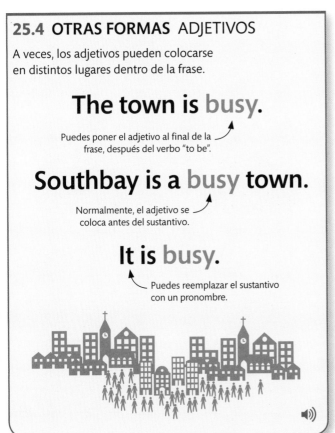

Aa 25.5 LEE EL FRAGMENTO Y SEÑALA LOS SIETE ADJETIVOS

Hi! I'm Paolo.

I live and work in a (small) town. There are some beautiful old buildings there and lots of hotels, too. I work in a large restaurant near the river. I'm a waiter and my friend is the chef. The restaurant is busy every evening and my job is horrible, but the food is beautiful. I eat there every day.

25.6 COMPLETA LOS ESPACIOS Y ESCRIBE CADA FRASE DE TRES MANERAS DISTINTAS

Rome is an old city.	The city is old.	It is old.
❶ She is a busy nurse.		
❷ He is a quiet dog.		
❸ They are new patients.		
❹ It is a horrible town.		
❺ It is a beautiful car.		

25.7 VOCABULARIO LUGARES Y PAISAJES

beach

sea

sand

grass

countryside

tree

hill

river

mountain

lake

sky

cloud

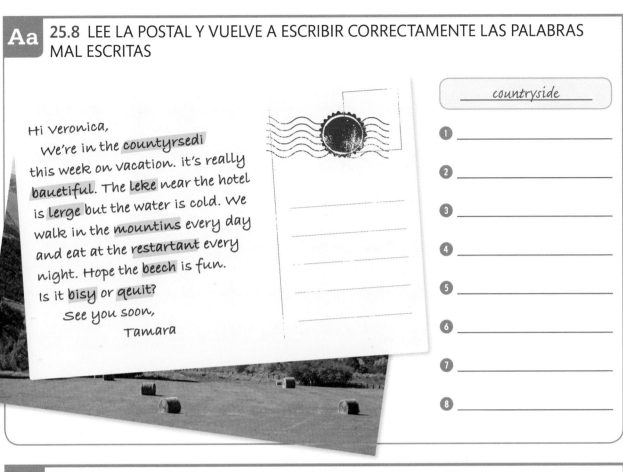

Aa 25.8 LEE LA POSTAL Y VUELVE A ESCRIBIR CORRECTAMENTE LAS PALABRAS MAL ESCRITAS

Hi Veronica,
We're in the countyrsedi this week on vacation. It's really bauetiful. The leke near the hotel is lerge but the water is cold. We walk in the mountins every day and eat at the restartant every night. Hope the beech is fun.
Is it bisy or qeuit?
See you soon,
Tamara

_____countryside_____

1 _____

2 _____

3 _____

4 _____

5 _____

6 _____

7 _____

8 _____

25.9 DI LAS FRASES EN VOZ ALTA, COMPLETANDO LOS ESPACIOS

The lakes _are_ beautiful _and the_ mountain _is_ large.

1 _____ countryside _____ quiet _____ trees _____ beautiful.

2 _____ city _____ horrible _____ people _____ busy.

3 _____ hotel _____ new _____ swimming pool _____ large.

4 _____ beach _____ big _____ cafés _____ busy.

5 _____ city _____ old _____ buildings _____ beautiful.

25.10 PUNTO CLAVE UTILIZAR EXPRESIONES CUANTITATIVAS

El inglés dispone de diferentes expresiones para cuantificar cuando se desconoce la cantidad exacta.

Utiliza "some" cuando hay más de uno, pero no sabes exactamente cuántos.

There are some buildings.

Utiliza "a few" cuando son pocos.

There are a few buildings.

Utiliza "lots of" cuando son muchos.

There are lots of buildings.

25.11 MÁS EJEMPLOS UTILIZAR EXPRESIONES CUANTITATIVAS

 There are some trees.

There are lots of people.

 There are lots of mountains.

There are a few cars.

25.12 ESCUCHA EL AUDIO Y LUEGO NUMERA LAS IMÁGENES EN EL ORDEN EN QUE SE DESCRIBEN

25.13 ESCRIBE FRASES A PARTIR DE LA IMAGEN, UTILIZANDO "A FEW", "SOME" O "LOTS OF"

_____There are some_____ trees.

❶ _____ people.

❷ _____ buildings.

❸ _____ cars.

❹ _____ parks.

25.14 OBSERVA LA TABLA Y DI FRASES EN VOZ ALTA UTILIZANDO "A FEW", "SOME" O "LOTS OF"

	A FEW	SOME	LOTS OF
In Greenpoint,	🏠		🚶
❶ In the tree,	🐦	🍎	
❷ In the sea,	🚶		🐟
❸ In the countryside,		🚶	🌲

In Greenpoint, there are a few buildings and lots of people.

25 ✓ CHECKLIST

⚙ Adjetivos ☐   **Aa** Adjetivos y nombres de lugares ☐   🧩 Describir lugares ☐

26 Dar razones

Utiliza la conjunción "because" para explicar la causa de algo. También puedes utilizar "because" para responder a la pregunta "why?".

🔧 **Lenguaje** "Because"
Aa **Vocabulario** Lugares y trabajos
🧩 **Habilidad** Dar razones

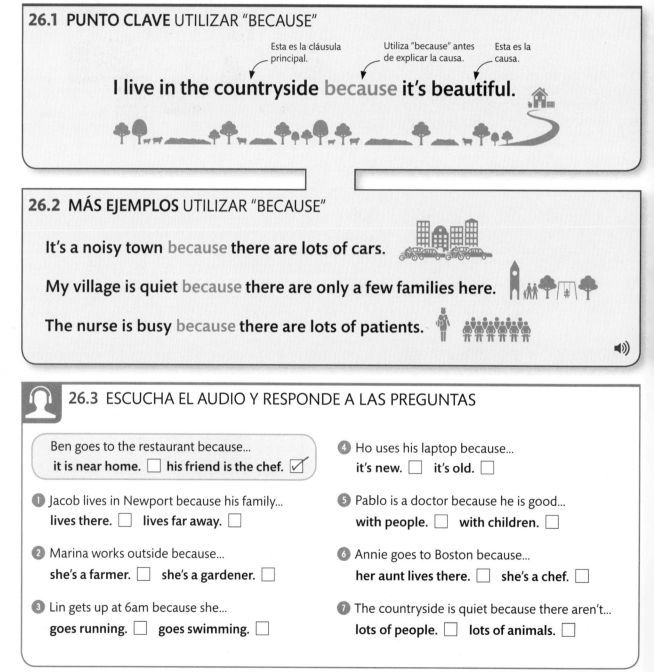

26.1 PUNTO CLAVE UTILIZAR "BECAUSE"

Esta es la cláusula principal.

Utiliza "because" antes de explicar la causa.

Esta es la causa.

I live in the countryside because it's beautiful.

26.2 MÁS EJEMPLOS UTILIZAR "BECAUSE"

It's a noisy town because there are lots of cars.

My village is quiet because there are only a few families here.

The nurse is busy because there are lots of patients.

26.3 ESCUCHA EL AUDIO Y RESPONDE A LAS PREGUNTAS

Ben goes to the restaurant because...
it is near home. ☐ **his friend is the chef.** ☑

1 Jacob lives in Newport because his family...
lives there. ☐ **lives far away.** ☐

2 Marina works outside because...
she's a farmer. ☐ **she's a gardener.** ☐

3 Lin gets up at 6am because she...
goes running. ☐ **goes swimming.** ☐

4 Ho uses his laptop because...
it's new. ☐ **it's old.** ☐

5 Pablo is a doctor because he is good...
with people. ☐ **with children.** ☐

6 Annie goes to Boston because...
her aunt lives there. ☐ **she's a chef.** ☐

7 The countryside is quiet because there aren't...
lots of people. ☐ **lots of animals.** ☐

26.4 COMPLETA LOS ESPACIOS UTILIZANDO LAS FRASES DEL RECUADRO

I work in a theater because ___*I'm an actor*___ .

1 She lives on a farm because _____ .

2 She works in a hotel because _____ .

3 They get up late because _____ .

4 We work with children because _____ .

5 You don't eat lunch because _____ .

6 I work outside because _____ .

7 My parents go to the countryside because _____ .

I'm a gardener

we're teachers

~~I'm an actor~~

you're busy

she's a farmer

they're students

it's quiet

she's a receptionist

🔊

---

26 ✓ CHECKLIST

⚙ "Because" ☐   **Aa** Lugares y trabajos ☐   🧩 Dar razones ☐

♻ REPASA LO QUE HAS APRENDIDO EN LAS UNIDADES 20–26

NUEVO LENGUAJE	FRASES DE EJEMPLO	☑	UNIDAD
UTILIZAR "THERE IS" Y "THERE ARE"	There is a hospital. There are three hospitals. There isn't a school. There aren't any schools.	☐	21.1, 21.6
ARTÍCULOS	I work in a library. I work in the library on Main Street.	☐	22.1
UTILIZAR "ANY" Y "SOME"	Are there any hotels? There are some hotels.	☐	22.8
IMPERATIVO	Stop! Be careful!	☐	23.1
UNIR FRASES	There's a library and a restaurant. There's a hotel, but there isn't a store.	☐	24.1, 24.7
UTILIZAR ADJETIVOS	She is a busy woman. It is a busy town. The town is busy. It is busy.	☐	25.1, 25.4
UTILIZAR "BECAUSE"	I live in the countryside because it's beautiful.	☐	26.1

27 Vocabulario

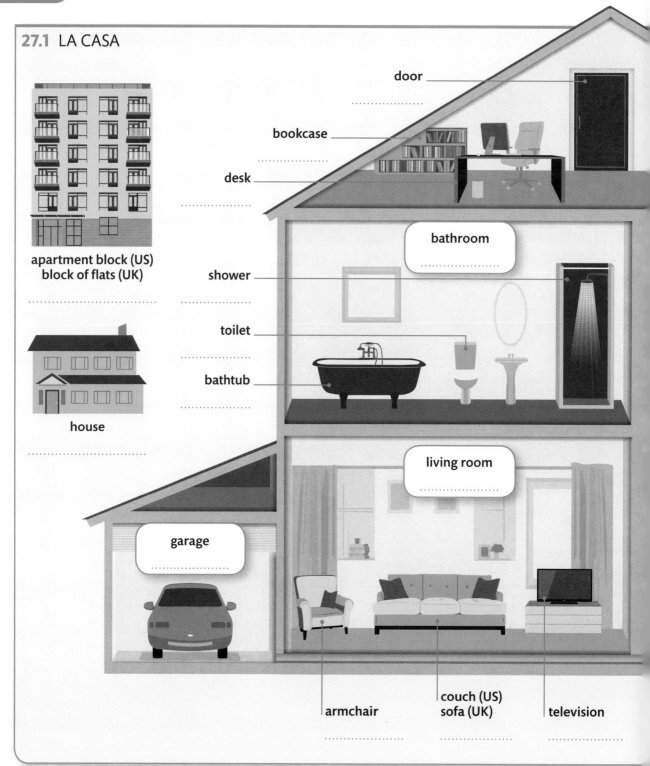

27.1 LA CASA

apartment block (US)
block of flats (UK)

house

door

bookcase

desk

bathroom

shower

toilet

bathtub

garage

living room

armchair

couch (US)
sofa (UK)

television

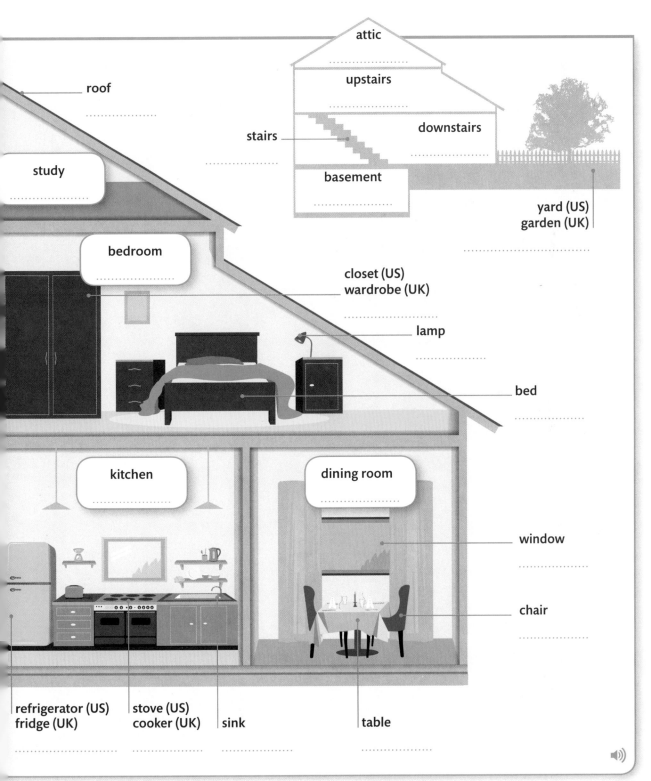

attic

upstairs

roof

downstairs

stairs

study

basement

yard (US)
garden (UK)

bedroom

closet (US)
wardrobe (UK)

lamp

bed

kitchen

dining room

window

chair

refrigerator (US)
fridge (UK)

stove (US)
cooker (UK)

sink

table

101

28 Mis cosas

Cuando hables de tus cosas, como por ejemplo muebles o mascotas, puedes utilizar el verbo "have". También lo puedes usar para referirte a tus cualidades y a los electrodomésticos y habitaciones de tu casa.

⚙ **Lenguaje** Utilizar "have"

Aa Vocabulario Objetos de la casa

🧩 **Habilidad** Hablar de las pertenencias

28.1 PUNTO CLAVE UTILIZAR "HAVE"

"Have" es un verbo irregular. La tercera persona del singular es "has", no "haves".

Utiliza "has" para la tercera persona del singular ("he", "she" o "it").

I have **a garage.**

She has **a yard.**

🔊

28.2 CÓMO FUNCIONA AFIRMACIONES USANDO "HAVE"

A estos pronombres les corresponde la forma verbal "have".

A estos pronombres les corresponde la forma verbal "has".

SUJETO	"HAVE"	OBJETO
I You We They	have	a garage.
He She It	has	

28.3 COMPLETA LOS ESPACIOS UTILIZANDO "HAVE" O "HAS"

I ___*have*___ a house.

① They _____ a car.

② You _____ a chair.

③ He _____ a dog.

④ We _____ a daughter.

⑤ It _____ a door.

🔊

28.4 ESCUCHA EL AUDIO Y MARCA A QUIÉN PERTENECE CADA OBJETO

Maya ✓ Ben ☐

① Maya ☐ Ben ☐

② Maya ☐ Ben ☐

③ Maya ☐ Ben ☐

④ Maya ☐ Ben ☐

28.5 LEE LOS ANUNCIOS Y RESPONDE A LAS PREGUNTAS

Riverside Apartment has four bedrooms.
True ☐ **False** ✓

① Riverside Apartment has one bathroom.
True ☐ **False** ☐

② Lake View has a yard.
True ☐ **False** ☐

③ Lake View has a garage.
True ☐ **False** ☐

④ Stone Hill has five bedrooms.
True ☐ **False** ☐

⑤ Stone Hill has a shower.
True ☐ **False** ☐

⑥ Stone Hill has a kitchen.
True ☐ **False** ☐

34 ACCOMMODATION

PROPERTIES TO RENT

Riverside Apartment $800/month
This old apartment is on the first floor of Riverside House. It has three bedrooms and two bathrooms. There's a beautiful park next door.

Lake View $900/month
This house is on a quiet street next to a lake. It has two bedrooms and a big kitchen in the basement. It also has a beautiful yard, but there is no garage.

Stone Hill $1,500/month
This house is in the old part of Bridgewater. It has four bedrooms and a bathroom with a bathtub and a shower. It also has a big kitchen. All the furniture is new and stylish.

28.6 PUNTO CLAVE FRASES NEGATIVAS CON "HAVE"

Aunque "have" es un verbo irregular, la forma negativa se construye de la manera habitual. Como en otros verbos, la forma negativa también puede contraerse.

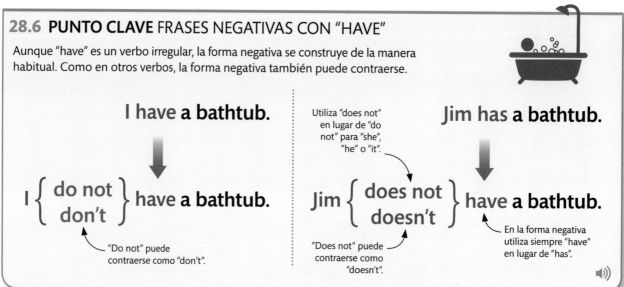

I have **a bathtub.**

I { **do not** / **don't** } have **a bathtub.**

"Do not" puede contraerse como "don't".

Utiliza "does not" en lugar de "do not" para "she", "he" o "it".

Jim has **a bathtub.**

Jim { **does not** / **doesn't** } have **a bathtub.**

"Does not" puede contraerse como "doesn't".

En la forma negativa utiliza siempre "have" en lugar de "has".

28.7 ESCRIBE LA FORMA NEGATIVA DE CADA FRASE

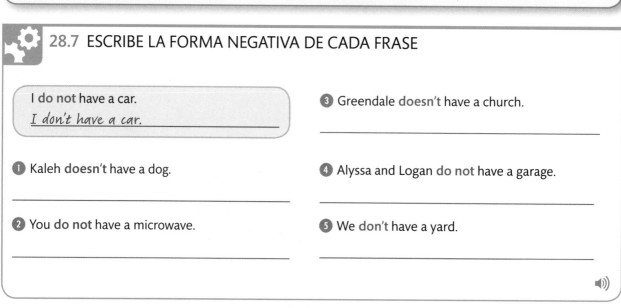

I do not have a car.
I don't have a car.

1 Kaleh **doesn't** have a dog.

_____

2 You **do not** have a microwave.

_____

3 Greendale **doesn't** have a church.

_____

4 Alyssa and Logan **do not** have a garage.

_____

5 We **don't** have a yard.

_____

28.8 USA EL DIAGRAMA PARA CREAR 11 FRASES CORRECTAS Y DILAS EN VOZ ALTA

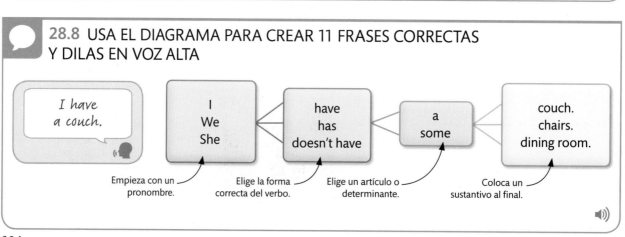

I have a couch.

| I / We / She | have / has / doesn't have | a / some | couch. / chairs. / dining room. |

Empieza con un pronombre.

Elige la forma correcta del verbo.

Elige un artículo o determinante.

Coloca un sustantivo al final.

28.9 OTRAS FORMAS "HAVE"

Algunos anglohablantes, especialmente en el Reino Unido, utilizan "have got" en lugar de "have", pero significa lo mismo.

We $\left\{ \begin{array}{l} \text{have} \\ \text{have got} \end{array} \right\}$ a dog.

La única diferencia es la palabra "got".

28.10 CÓMO FUNCIONA "HAVE GOT"

POSITIVO	NEGATIVO
I have got a dog.	He has not got a dog.
I've got a dog.	He hasn't got a dog.

Usa esta forma tan solo cuando utilices "have" con "got". No contraigas "I have" como "I've a dog".

"Has not got" puede contraerse como "hasn't got".

28.11 ESCRIBE LAS OTRAS DOS VARIANTES DE CADA FRASE

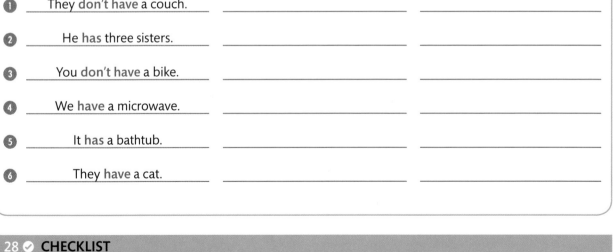

	She has a computer.	She has got a computer.	She's got a computer.
1	They don't have a couch.		
2	He has three sisters.		
3	You don't have a bike.		
4	We have a microwave.		
5	It has a bathtub.		
6	They have a cat.		

28 ✓ CHECKLIST

⚙ Utilizar "have" ☐   **Aa** Objetos de la casa ☐   Hablar de las pertenencias ☐

29 ¿Qué tienes?

Haz preguntas con "have" para averiguar las cosas que posee alguien. Los auxiliares "do" o "does" ayudan a formar la pregunta.

⚙ **Lenguaje** Preguntas con "have"

Aa Vocabulario La casa y los muebles

🧩 **Habilidad** Preguntar sobre objetos de casa

29.1 PUNTO CLAVE HACER PREGUNTAS CON "HAVE"

Para hacer preguntas con "have", debes utilizar "do" o "does".

En las preguntas "has" pasa a ser "have".

You have a TV.

⬇

Do you have a TV?

Con los pronombres "I", "you" y "we" añade "do" para convertir las frases afirmativas en preguntas.

She has a TV.

⬇

Does she have a TV?

Con los pronombres "he", "she" o "it" añade "does" para hacer preguntas.

🔊

29.2 VOCABULARIO OBJETOS DE CASA

toaster

microwave

washing machine

dishwasher

kettle

plate

bowl

cup

silverware (US)
cutlery (UK)

knife

fork

spoon

🔊

29.3 REESCRIBE LAS FRASES COMO PREGUNTAS

She has an oven.
Does she have an oven?

1 They have a toaster.
_____

2 You have a new couch.
_____

3 Ben has a washing machine.
_____

4 We have an old armchair.
_____

5 Karen has a large TV.
_____

6 The kitchen has a sink.
_____

7 The house has a yard.
_____

29.4 ESCUCHA EL AUDIO Y MARCA A QUIÉN PERTENECEN LOS OBJETOS

Tim ☑ Lucy ☐

3 Tim ☐ Lucy ☐

1 Tim ☐ Lucy ☐

4 Tim ☐ Lucy ☐

2 Tim ☐ Lucy ☐

5 Tim ☐ Lucy ☐

29.5 USA EL DIAGRAMA PARA CREAR 9 FRASES CORRECTAS Y DILAS EN VOZ ALTA

Do you have any chairs?

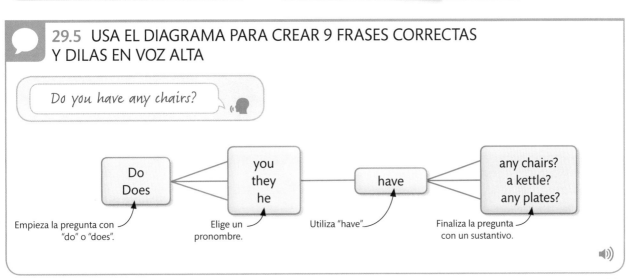

| Do / Does | you / they / he | have | any chairs? / a kettle? / any plates? |

Empieza la pregunta con "do" o "does".

Elige un pronombre.

Utiliza "have".

Finaliza la pregunta con un sustantivo.

29.6 PUNTO CLAVE RESPUESTAS CORTAS A LAS PREGUNTAS CON "HAVE"

Puedes dar respuestas cortas a las preguntas con "have" utilizando "do" y "don't".

Añade "do" para hacer una pregunta.

Do you have **a microwave?**

Utiliza "do" en las respuestas afirmativas.

Yes, I do.

No, I don't.

Utiliza "do not" o "don't" en las respuestas negativas.

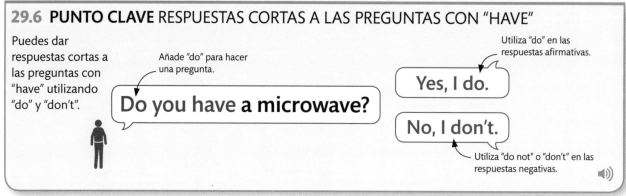

29.7 OBSERVA EL DIBUJO Y RESPONDE A LAS PREGUNTAS CON RESPUESTAS CORTAS

Do you have a kettle?

Yes, I do.

❶ Do you have a fork?

_____

❷ Do you have a spoon?

_____

❸ Do you have a toaster?

_____

❹ Do you have a microwave?

_____

29.8 OBSERVA EL DIBUJO Y RESPONDE A LAS PREGUNTAS EN VOZ ALTA

Does Noah have a dog?

Yes, he does.

❶ Does he have a TV?

❷ Does he have a bookcase?

❸ Does he have a couch?

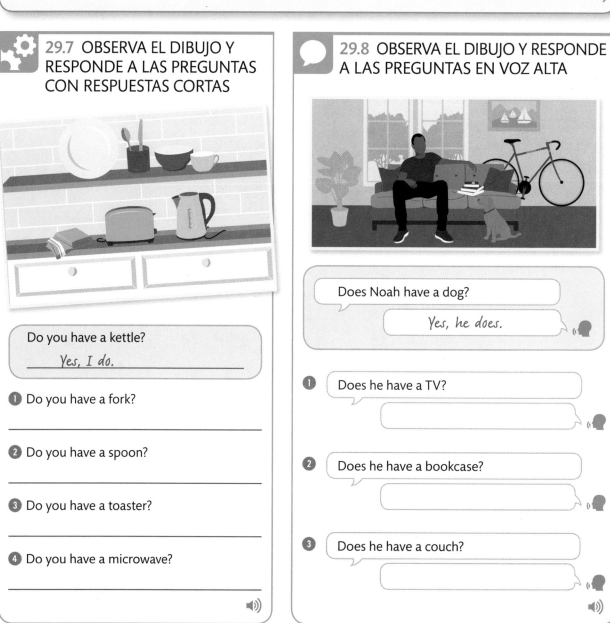

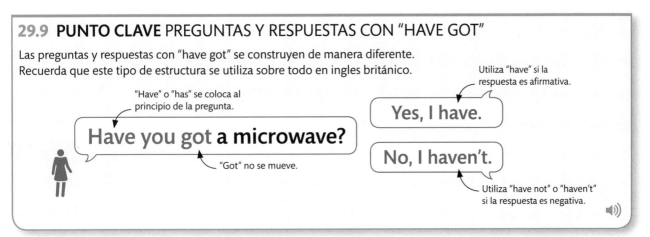

29.9 PUNTO CLAVE PREGUNTAS Y RESPUESTAS CON "HAVE GOT"

Las preguntas y respuestas con "have got" se construyen de manera diferente.
Recuerda que este tipo de estructura se utiliza sobre todo en ingles británico.

"Have" o "has" se coloca al principio de la pregunta.

Utiliza "have" si la respuesta es afirmativa.

Have you got a microwave?

"Got" no se mueve.

Yes, I have.

No, I haven't.

Utiliza "have not" o "haven't" si la respuesta es negativa.

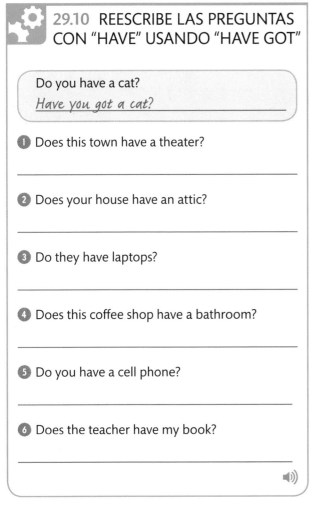

29.10 REESCRIBE LAS PREGUNTAS CON "HAVE" USANDO "HAVE GOT"

Do you have a cat?
Have you got a cat?

① Does this town have a theater?

_____

② Does your house have an attic?

_____

③ Do they have laptops?

_____

④ Does this coffee shop have a bathroom?

_____

⑤ Do you have a cell phone?

_____

⑥ Does the teacher have my book?

_____

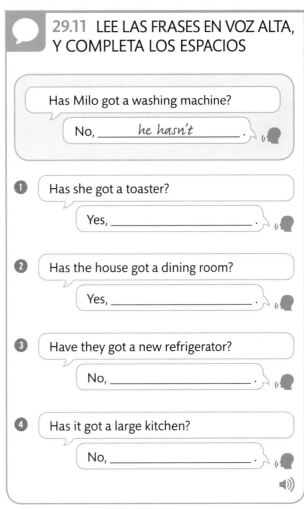

29.11 LEE LAS FRASES EN VOZ ALTA, Y COMPLETA LOS ESPACIOS

Has Milo got a washing machine?

No, ___ _he hasn't_ ___ .

① Has she got a toaster?

Yes, _____ .

② Has the house got a dining room?

Yes, _____ .

③ Have they got a new refrigerator?

No, _____ .

④ Has it got a large kitchen?

No, _____ .

29 ✓ CHECKLIST

⚙ Preguntas con "have" ☐   **Aa** La casa y los muebles ☐   🧩 Preguntar sobre objetos de casa ☐

30 Vocabulario

30.1 COMIDA Y BEBIDA

food

drinks

breakfast

lunch

dinner

meat

fish

seafood

fruit

vegetables

bread

pasta

rice

noodles

potatoes

milk

cheese

butter

yogurt

eggs

sugar

cookie (US)
biscuit (UK)

chocolate

cake

cereal

orange

apple

banana

strawberry

mango

sandwich

burger

fries (US)
chips (UK)

spaghetti

salad

coffee

tea

juice

water

lemonade

31 Contar

En inglés, los sustantivos pueden ser contables e incontables. Los contables se pueden contar individualmente. Los objetos que no se pueden contar por separado se llaman incontables.

⚙ **Lenguaje** Sustantivos incontables
Aa Vocabulario Contenedores de comida
🧩 **Habilidad** Hablar sobre la comida

31.1 PUNTO CLAVE SUSTANTIVOS CONTABLES E INCONTABLES

Utiliza "a", "an", o un número para hablar de sustantivos contables.
Utiliza "some" para sustantivos contables e incontables.

SUSTANTIVOS CONTABLES

There is an egg.

There are four eggs.

There are some eggs.

Utiliza "some" cuando hay más objetos contables de los que puedes contar con facilidad.

SUSTANTIVOS INCONTABLES

Los sustantivos incontables van siempre con el verbo en singular.

There is some rice.

Con sustantivos incontables utiliza siempre "some". No uses "a", "an" o un número.

31.2 MÁS EJEMPLOS SUSTANTIVOS CONTABLES E INCONTABLES

 a **sandwich**   an **apple**

 four **bananas**   two **burgers**

 some **milk**   some **water**

 some **spaghetti**   some **sugar**

31.3 TACHA LA PALABRA INCORRECTA DE CADA FRASE

Michael has ~~two~~ / some milk.

❶ Jake has an / some apple.

❷ There is a / some coffee.

❸ Reena eats a / some spaghetti.

❹ There are two / some eggs.

❺ I've got a / some bananas.

31.4 PUNTO CLAVE LA FORMA NEGATIVA Y LAS PREGUNTAS

Tanto para los sustantivos contables como para los incontables, utiliza "any" para formar frases negativas e interrogativas.

SUSTANTIVOS CONTABLES	SUSTANTIVOS INCONTABLES
There are some eggs.	**There is some rice.**
Utiliza "are" para frases contables afirmativas.	Utiliza "is" para frases incontables afirmativas.
There aren't any eggs.	**There isn't any rice.**
Utiliza "aren't" para frases contables negativas.	Utiliza "isn't" para frases incontables negativas.
Are there any eggs?	**Is there any rice?**
Utiliza "are there" para preguntas contables.	Utiliza "is there" para preguntas incontables.

◀))

31.5 COMPLETA LOS ESPACIOS CON AFIRMACIONES Y PREGUNTAS

Are there any bananas?	*There are some bananas.*	*There aren't any bananas.*
❶ Is there any milk?		
❷	There is some chocolate.	
❸		There aren't any apples.

31.6 RESPONDE A LAS PREGUNTAS COMPLETANDO LOS ESPACIOS Y DILAS EN VOZ ALTA

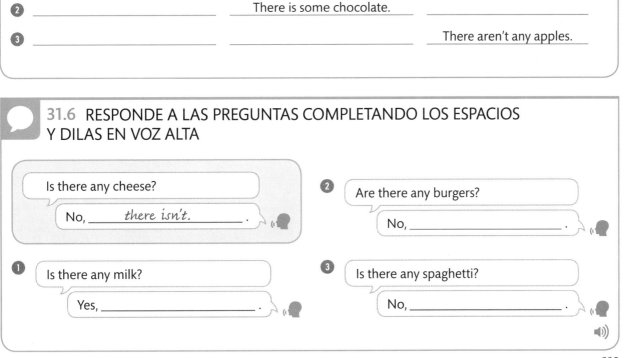

Is there any cheese?

No, _____*there isn't.*_____ .

❷ Are there any burgers?

No, _____ .

❶ Is there any milk?

Yes, _____ .

❸ Is there any spaghetti?

No, _____ .

◀))

113

31.7 VOCABULARIO CONTENEDORES DE ALIMENTOS

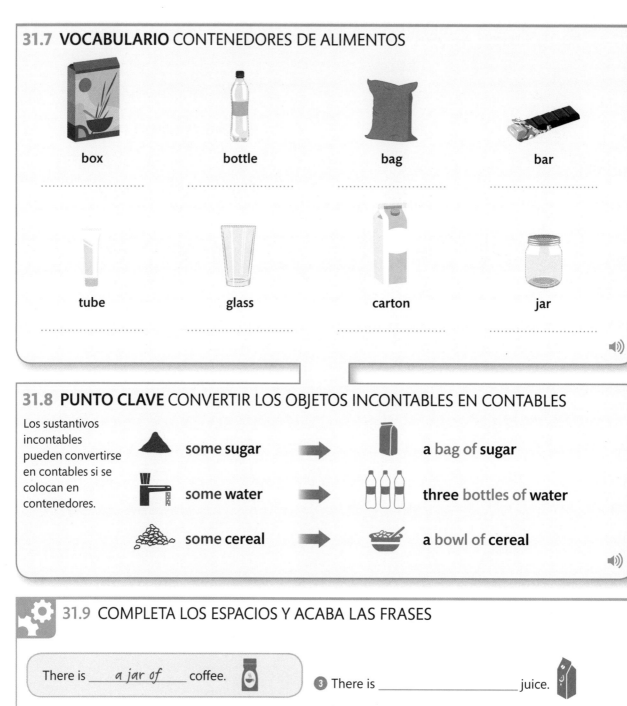

box ....

bottle ....

bag ....

bar ....

tube ....

glass ....

carton ....

jar ....

31.8 PUNTO CLAVE CONVERTIR LOS OBJETOS INCONTABLES EN CONTABLES

Los sustantivos incontables pueden convertirse en contables si se colocan en contenedores.

some sugar ➡ a bag of sugar

some water ➡ three bottles of water

some cereal ➡ a bowl of cereal

31.9 COMPLETA LOS ESPACIOS Y ACABA LAS FRASES

There is _____a jar of_____ coffee.

❶ There is _____ flour.

❷ There is _____ coffee.

❸ There is _____ juice.

❹ There are _____ spaghetti.

❺ There are _____ milk.

31.10 PUNTO CLAVE PREGUNTAS SOBRE CANTIDADES

Utiliza "many" para preguntar las cantidades de los sustantivos contables
y "much" en el caso de los sustantivos incontables.

How many eggs are there?

Utiliza "many" para las
preguntas contables.

How much rice is there?

Utiliza "much" para las
preguntas incontables.

31.11 MÁS EJEMPLOS PREGUNTAS SOBRE CANTIDADES

How many cupcakes are there?

How many apples are there?

How much pasta is there?

How much chocolate is there?

31.12 COMPLETA LOS ESPACIOS CON "HOW MUCH" Y "HOW MANY"

_____How much_____ pizza is there?

1 _____ glasses of juice are there?

2 _____ water is there?

3 _____ potatoes are there?

4 _____ bars of chocolate are there?

5 _____ pasta is there?

6 _____ cartons of juice are there?

7 _____ milk is there?

31.13 ESCUCHA EL AUDIO Y RESPONDE A LAS PREGUNTAS

Escucha cómo Mila y Jon
planean ir de compras.

How many pizzas are there?
one ☐   **two** ☑   **three** ☐

1 How much flour do they need?
two bags ☐   **one bag** ☐   **three bags** ☐

2 How many cartons of juice are there?
one ☐   **three** ☐   **five** ☐

3 How much coffee is there?
none ☐   **some** ☐

4 They need some...
sausages ☐   **cheese** ☐   **burgers.** ☐

32 Medir

Utiliza "enough" cuando tengas la cantidad correcta de algún objeto. Utiliza "too many" o "too much" cuando tengas más que suficiente.

⚙️ **Lenguaje** Medidas
Aa Vocabulario Ingredientes y cantidades
🧩 **Habilidad** Hablar de cantidades

32.1 PUNTO CLAVE "ENOUGH / TOO MANY"

Utiliza "enough", "not enough", y "too many" para hablar sobre cantidades de sustantivos contables.

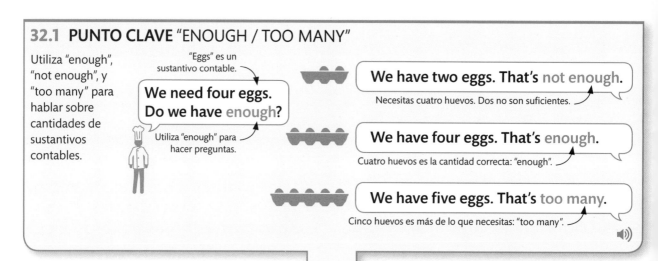

"Eggs" es un sustantivo contable.

We need four eggs. Do we have enough?

Utiliza "enough" para hacer preguntas.

We have two eggs. That's not enough.
Necesitas cuatro huevos. Dos no son suficientes.

We have four eggs. That's enough.
Cuatro huevos es la cantidad correcta: "enough".

We have five eggs. That's too many.
Cinco huevos es más de lo que necesitas: "too many".

32.2 MÁS EJEMPLOS "ENOUGH / TOO MANY"

There are enough **eggs.**

You have enough **eggs.**

There aren't enough **eggs.**

You don't **have** enough **eggs.**

There are too many **eggs.**

You have too many **eggs.**

32.3 LEE LA RECETA Y TACHA LAS PALABRAS INCORRECTAS DE CADA FRASE

There ~~aren't enough~~ / are too many mangoes.

FRUIT SALAD RECIPE
2 apples
4 oranges
1 pineapple
3 bananas
1 mango

1️⃣ There aren't enough / are enough oranges.

2️⃣ You have enough / too many pineapples.

3️⃣ There aren't enough / are too many apples.

4️⃣ You don't have enough / too many bananas.

32.4 PUNTO CLAVE "ENOUGH / TOO MUCH"

Utiliza "enough", "not enough" y "too much" para hablar sobre cantidades de sustantivos incontables.

We need eight ounces of flour. Do we have enough?

4oz
not enough **flour**

8oz
enough **flour**

12oz
too much **flour**

Necesitas ocho onzas: cuatro no son suficientes.

Ocho onzas es la cantidad suficiente: "enough".

Doce onzas es más de lo que necesitas: "too much".

32.5 MÁS EJEMPLOS "ENOUGH / TOO MUCH"

There is enough **flour.**

They have enough **flour.**

There isn't enough **flour.**

They don't **have** enough **flour.**

There is too much **flour.**

They have too much **flour.**

32.6 ESCUCHA Y CONECTA LOS DIBUJOS CON LAS CANTIDADES

Sheila y Vikram preparan los ingredientes para hacer un pastel.

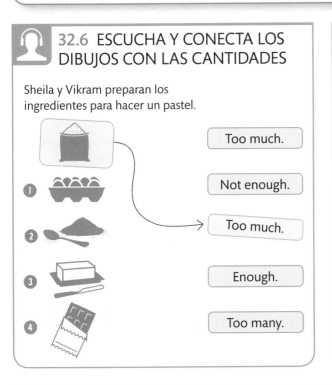

Too much.

Not enough.

Too much.

Enough.

Too many.

32.7 TACHA LAS PALABRAS INCORRECTAS DE CADA FRASE

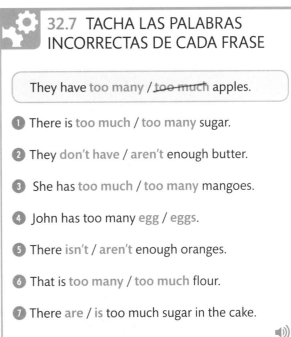

They have too many / ~~too much~~ apples.

1 There is too much / too many sugar.

2 They don't have / aren't enough butter.

3 She has too much / too many mangoes.

4 John has too many egg / eggs.

5 There isn't / aren't enough oranges.

6 That is too many / too much flour.

7 There are / is too much sugar in the cake.

32 ✔ CHECKLIST

⚙ Medidas ☐   **Aa** Ingredientes y cantidades ☐   Hablar de cantidades ☐

33.1 ROPA Y ACCESORIOS

t-shirt

blouse

shirt

dress

skirt

pants (US)
trousers (UK)

jeans

jacket

coat

raincoat

socks

boots

shoes

sandals

sneakers (US)
trainers (UK)

scarf

hat

gloves

belt

purse (US)
handbag (UK)

33.2 TALLAS DE ROPA

extra small
....

small
....

medium
....

large
....

extra large
....

33.3 DESCRIBIR LA ROPA

smart
....

casual
....

suit
....

uniform
....

short sleeves
....

long sleeves
....

cheap
....

expensive
....

33.4 COLORES: "COLORS" (ESTADOS UNIDOS) / "COLOURS" (REINO UNIDO)

red
....

orange
....

yellow
....

green
....

blue
....

purple
....

pink
....

white
....

gray (US)
grey (UK)
....

black
....

34 De compras

Puedes utilizar varios verbos para hablar sobre lo que pasa cuando vas de compras. Utiliza "too" y "enough" para describir cómo te queda la ropa.

⚙ **Lenguaje** Utilizar "too" y "fit"
Aa Vocabulario Compras y ropa
🧩 **Habilidad** Describir la ropa

34.1 VOCABULARIO VERBOS RELACIONADOS CON COMPRAR

Ana owns a red hat.

Choose a new shirt!

Luc sells old clothes.

They want new shoes.

The hat fits Jane.

Let's buy some hats!

 34.2 TACHA LA PALABRA INCORRECTA DE CADA FRASE

Tsuru ~~want~~ / **wants** a green jumper.

❶ Hannah **choose** / **chooses** a yellow skirt.

❷ Elliot and Ruby **buy** / **buys** a new couch.

❸ Sue **own** / **owns** an old winter coat.

❹ Jess's dad **buy** / **buys** her a new bike.

❺ Chris and Lisa **own** / **owns** a black sports car.

❻ Gayle and Mike **sell** / **sells** shoes at the market.

❼ Mia **choose** / **chooses** her red shoes.

❽ The shoes **fit** / **fits** me.

❾ We **want** / **wants** new white shirts.

34.3 VUELVE A ESCRIBIR LAS FRASES PONIENDO LAS PALABRAS EN SU ORDEN CORRECTO

She | a | green | long | dress | buys

She buys a long green dress.

① They | expensive | sweaters. | blue | choose

_____

② some | brown | old | hats. | has | Judith

_____

③ sells | This | shop | short | red | pants.

_____

④ owns | Tina | black | cheap | shoes.

_____

⑤ Jim | buys | black | new | a | coat

_____

34.4 LEE LOS MENSAJES Y MARCA 12 ADJETIVOS

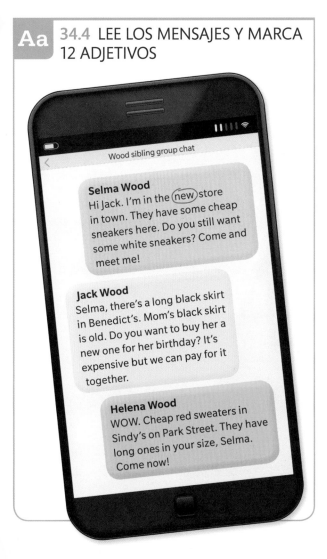

Wood sibling group chat

Selma Wood
Hi Jack. I'm in the (new) store in town. They have some cheap sneakers here. Do you still want some white sneakers? Come and meet me!

Jack Wood
Selma, there's a long black skirt in Benedict's. Mom's black skirt is old. Do you want to buy her a new one for her birthday? It's expensive but we can pay for it together.

Helena Wood
WOW. Cheap red sweaters in Sindy's on Park Street. They have long ones in your size, Selma. Come now!

34.5 ESCUCHA EL AUDIO Y RESPONDE A LAS PREGUNTAS

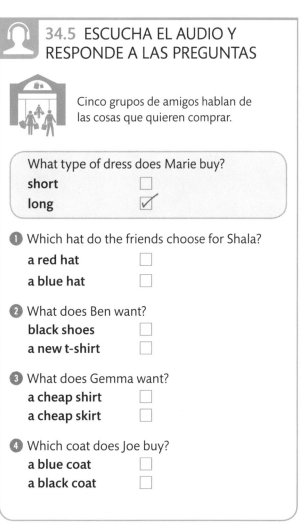

Cinco grupos de amigos hablan de las cosas que quieren comprar.

What type of dress does Marie buy?
short ☐
long ☑

① Which hat do the friends choose for Shala?
a red hat ☐
a blue hat ☐

② What does Ben want?
black shoes ☐
a new t-shirt ☐

③ What does Gemma want?
a cheap shirt ☐
a cheap skirt ☐

④ Which coat does Joe buy?
a blue coat ☐
a black coat ☐

121

34.6 PUNTO CLAVE RESPONDER A LA PREGUNTA: "DOES IT FIT?"

En inglés, se utiliza "enough" y "too" con adjetivos para describir si una prenda de ropa te queda bien.

El sustantivo se coloca delante cuando la pregunta es acerca de la talla correcta.

Does the sweater fit?

No, it is not big enough.

Is the sweater too small?

No, it is big enough.

Does the sweater fit?

No, it is too big.

34.7 CONECTA LAS FRASES QUE SIGNIFICAN LO MISMO

not big enough	too old
① not expensive enough	too small
② not cheap enough	too cheap
③ not short enough	too short
④ not long enough	too expensive
⑤ not new enough	too long
⑥ not old enough	too big
⑦ not small enough	too new

34.8 COMPLETA CON LAS EXPRESIONES DEL RECUADRO

Lucy's blue coat is _____ *too big* _____.

① Jim's pants are _____.

② Sam's dress is _____.

③ Molly's sweater is _____.

④ Helen's red hat is _____.

⑤ Lili's shoes are _____.

~~too big~~	too long	too short
too small	too big	too big

34.9 ESCUCHA EL AUDIO Y MARCA LA PRENDA QUE DESCRIBE CADA PERSONA

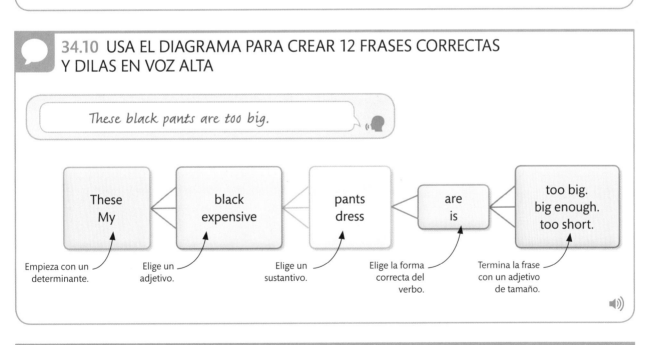

34.10 USA EL DIAGRAMA PARA CREAR 12 FRASES CORRECTAS Y DILAS EN VOZ ALTA

These black pants are *too big*.

| These My | black expensive | pants dress | are is | too big. big enough. too short. |

Empieza con un determinante.

Elige un adjetivo.

Elige un sustantivo.

Elige la forma correcta del verbo.

Termina la frase con un adjetivo de tamaño.

34 ✓ CHECKLIST

Utilizar "too" y "fit" ☐   **Aa** Compras y ropa ☐   Describir la ropa ☐

35 Describir cosas

Para dar tu opinión sobre alguna cosa o bien para facilitar información se pueden utilizar adjetivos. Antes de un sustantivo se puede colocar más de un adjetivo.

⚙ **Lenguaje** Adjetivos para opinar
Aa Vocabulario Ir de compras y materiales
🧩 **Habilidad** Dar opiniones

35.1 PUNTO CLAVE ADJETIVOS PARA OPINAR

Algunos adjetivos se utilizan para dar opiniones, no información.

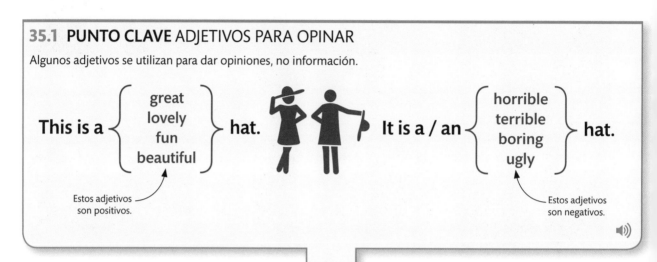

This is a { great / lovely / fun / beautiful } hat.

Estos adjetivos son positivos.

It is a / an { horrible / terrible / boring / ugly } hat.

Estos adjetivos son negativos.

35.2 PUNTO CLAVE ORDEN DE LOS ADJETIVOS

En inglés, los adjetivos suelen seguir un orden. Los que sirven para opinar se colocan antes que los utilizados para dar información.

	ADJETIVO DE OPINIÓN	ADJETIVO INFORMATIVO	SUSTANTIVO
This is a	lovely	green	hat.

Los adjetivos para dar opinión van primero.

Los adjetivos informativos se colocan al final.

35.3 MÁS EJEMPLOS EL ORDEN DE LOS ADJETIVOS

 It is a lovely big house.

 Natalie has a beautiful old cat.

 We have a horrible old car.

 They are ugly purple shoes.

 This is a great new book.

 He is a brilliant young actor.

35.4 TACHA EL ADJETIVO INCORRECTO DE CADA FRASE

It is a **good** / ~~bad~~ young dog.

❸ I have a **lovely** / **horrible** long dress.

❶ This is a **lovely** / **horrible** old t-shirt.

❹ This is a **beautiful** / **ugly** bird.

❷ This is a **boring** / **great** movie.

❺ This is a **fun** / **boring** party.

35.5 VUELVE A ESCRIBIR LAS FRASES PONIENDO LAS PALABRAS EN SU ORDEN CORRECTO

It is	bag.	beautiful	red	a

It is a beautiful red bag.

❶ | a | horrible | That is | blue car. |

_____

❷ | This is | fun | story. | short | a |

_____

❸ | have a | I | black | cat. | lovely |

_____

❹ | ugly | He has | red | an | house. |

_____

❺ | They own | a great | laptop. | new |

_____

35.6 ESCUCHA EL AUDIO Y MARCA LAS RESPUESTAS CORRECTAS

What does Rachel have?

❶ Which book is good?

❷ What class is boring?

❸ What does Ben have?

❹ Which piece of clothing is fun?

125

35.7 VOCABULARIO MATERIALES

Algunas palabras pueden utilizarse tanto como sustantivos para nombrar materiales o como adjetivos para decir de qué están hechos los objetos. Dos de los sustantivos siguientes cambian cuando se convierten en adjetivos: "wood" a "wooden", y "wool" a "woolen".

plastic

wood

glass

paper

wool

leather

metal

fabric

Aa 35.8 CONECTA LAS IMÁGENES CON SUS DESCRIPCIONES

Oh, no, the blue glass vase!

That's an expensive leather couch.

This is a beautiful wooden table.

What an interesting metal box!

We have two plastic chairs.

35.9 DI LAS FRASES EN VOZ ALTA CORRIGIENDO EL ORDEN DE LAS PALABRAS

We have lovely two purple couches.

We have two lovely purple couches.

1 She owns some wooden beautiful chairs.

2 We own don't those plastic plates horrible.

3 They have yellow an ugly car.

4 He wears a blue boring sweater.

5 She wants a metal lamp new.

6 He owns a fabric large bag.

7 Norah new a leather wants jacket.

---

35 ✓ CHECKLIST

⚙ Adjetivos para opinar ☐   **Aa** Ir de compras y materiales ☐   Dar opiniones ☐

↻ REPASA LO QUE HAS APRENDIDO EN LAS UNIDADES 27–35

NUEVO LENGUAJE	FRASES DE EJEMPLO	☑	UNIDAD
UTILIZAR "HAVE"	I have **a garage.** She has **a yard.** I do not **have a bathtub.**	☐	28.1, 28.6
FORMULAR PREGUNTAS CON "HAVE"	Do you have a TV?	☐	29.1
SUSTANTIVOS CONTABLES E INCONTABLES	**There are** four **eggs. There is** some **rice.** Are there any **eggs?** Is there any **rice?**	☐	31.1, 31.4
UTILIZAR "ENOUGH" Y "MANY"	**We have** enough **eggs.** **We have** too many **eggs.**	☐	32.1
VERBOS RELACIONADOS CON COMPRAR	**Ana** owns **a red hat. Luc** sells **old clothes.** **They** want **new shoes. The hat** fits **Jane.**	☐	34.1
ORDEN DE LOS ADJETIVOS	**This is a** lovely green **hat.**	☐	35.1

36.1 DEPORTES

swimming

sailing

skateboarding

running

skiing

snowboarding

roller-skating

surfing

tennis

golf

badminton

baseball

basketball

soccer (US)
football (UK)

football (US)
American
football (UK)

rugby

volleyball

cycling

ice hockey

horse riding

36.2 EQUIPO

baseball bat

tennis racket

golf club

ball

skateboard

skis

surfboard

snowboard

36.3 INSTALACIONES DEPORTIVAS

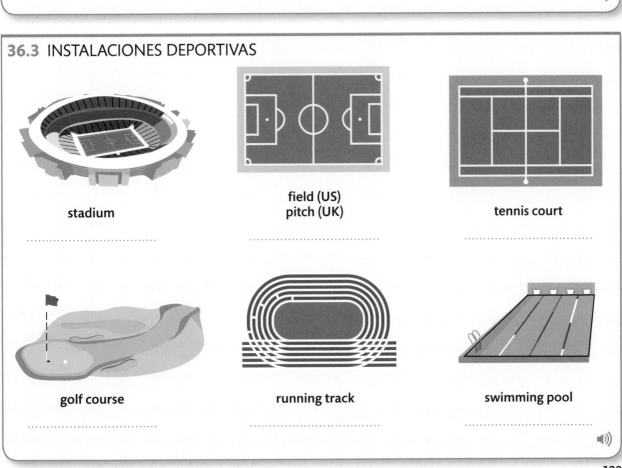

stadium

field (US)
pitch (UK)

tennis court

golf course

running track

swimming pool

37 Hablar sobre deportes

Para describir la práctica de algunos deportes, se utiliza el verbo "go" más el gerundio. Para otros deportes, se utiliza "play" más el sustantivo.

⚙ **Lenguaje** "Go" y "play"
Aa Vocabulario Deportes
🧩 **Habilidad** Hablar sobre deportes

37.1 PUNTO CLAVE "GO" CON UN GERUNDIO

Algunos verbos se convierten en sustantivos al añadir "ing" a la forma base del verbo. Reciben el nombre de gerundios. Muchos nombres de deportes son gerundios.

"Go" cambia con el sujeto.

She goes surfing on the weekend.

Añade "ing" a la forma base del verbo.

37.2 MÁS EJEMPLOS "GO" CON UN GERUNDIO

I go swimming once a week.

He goes skateboarding twice a month.

Do they go dancing on Saturday nights?

We don't go fishing at the lake.

He doesn't go cycling with his brothers.

Does she go sailing in the summer?

37.3 COMPLETA LOS ESPACIOS Y ACABA LAS FRASES

Tamara ____*goes*____ swimming in the sea.

 ❶ We don't _____ surfing in the winter.

 ❷ Do you _____ sailing on the weekend?

 ❸ Tipo _____ cycling five times a week.

❹ He _____ fishing on the river.

 ❺ Sharon _____ dancing with her friend.

 ❻ Do they _____ running every morning?

 ❼ He doesn't _____ horse riding.

37.4 ESCUCHA EL AUDIO Y UNE LOS DÍAS Y LOS DEPORTES QUE PRACTICA SAM

1 | | 2 | 3 | 4

Monday | Tuesday | Wednesday | Thursday | Friday

37.5 PUNTO CLAVE FORMACIÓN DE LOS GERUNDIOS

Los gerundios terminan en "ing" y se forman con estas sencillas reglas.

fish

go fishing

En la mayoría de los verbos, añade "ing".

Si el verbo termina en "e", elimínala.

skate

go skating

Añade entonces "ing".

En los verbos de una sílaba terminados en consonante + vocal + consonante...

swim

go swimming

... dobla la consonante final y añade "ing".

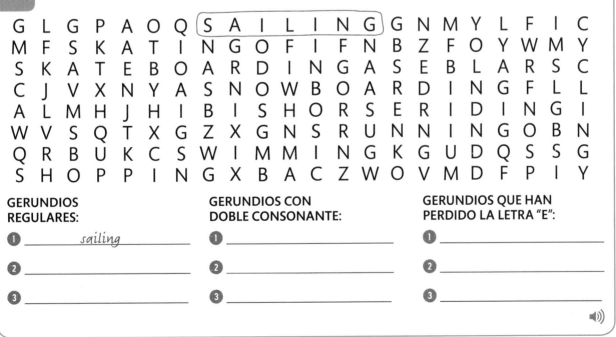

Aa **37.6 BUSCA NUEVE PALABRAS Y ESCRÍBELAS EN EL GRUPO CORRESPONDIENTE**

```
G L G P A O Q S A I L I N G G N M Y L F I C
M F S K A T I N G O F I F N B Z F O Y W M Y
S K A T E B O A R D I N G A S E B L A R S C
C J V X N Y A S N O W B O A R D I N G F L L
A L M H J H I B I S H O R S E R I D I N G I
W V S Q T X G Z X G N S R U N N I N G O B N
Q R B U K C S W I M M I N G K G U D Q S S G
S H O P P I N G X B A C Z W O V M D F P I Y
```

GERUNDIOS REGULARES:

1 _____ sailing _____

2 _____

3 _____

GERUNDIOS CON DOBLE CONSONANTE:

1 _____

2 _____

3 _____

GERUNDIOS QUE HAN PERDIDO LA LETRA "E":

1 _____

2 _____

3 _____

37.7 PUNTO CLAVE "PLAY" CON UN SUSTANTIVO

Para hablar sobre algunos deportes, especialmente juegos de pelota y competiciones, se utiliza "play" con el sustantivo.

"Play" cambia en función del sujeto.

El sustantivo se coloca después del verbo.

They play tennis on Sundays.

37.8 MÁS EJEMPLOS "PLAY" CON UN SUSTANTIVO

 I don't play tennis in winter.

 He plays baseball for the town.

 Does Dani play hockey on Mondays?

 Sala plays golf on Tuesday mornings.

 Do Ben and Si play chess together?

 We don't play badminton any more.

37.9 TACHA LA PALABRA INCORRECTA DE CADA FRASE

I ~~plays~~ / play football in the park.

1. Shala don't / doesn't play tennis.

2. Mina plays / play golf at the club.

3. We plays / play squash on Mondays.

4. The dog plays / play with its ball.

5. Maria don't / doesn't play tennis.

6. The kids don't / doesn't play games at school.

7. They play / plays soccer at the park.

37.10 VUELVE A ESCRIBIR LAS FRASES CORRIGIENDO LOS ERRORES

He **don't play** hockey in the summer.
He doesn't play hockey in the summer.

1. We **plays** tennis every Tuesday night.

_____

2. They **doesn't play** golf during the week.

_____

3. You **doesn't play** volleyball at the beach.

_____

4. Do they **plays** together every Saturday?

_____

37.11 LEE EL ARTÍCULO Y RESPONDE A LAS PREGUNTAS

Who plays squash on Mondays and Fridays?

James ✓ Sara ☐ Chas ☐ Cassie ☐

1 Who plays golf?

James ☐ Sara ☐ Chas ☐ Cassie ☐

2 Who goes running in the park?

James ☐ Sara ☐ Chas ☐ Cassie ☐

3 Who goes swimming on Thursdays?

James ☐ Sara ☐ Chas ☐ Cassie ☐

4 Who plays badminton?

James ☐ Sara ☐ Chas ☐ Cassie ☐

YOUR SPORTS

Littleton's Sports Scene

Some local residents tell us about their sports routines

I go to Belgrade Sports. It's a great place to exercise. I play squash on Mondays and Fridays.
JAMES

I love Highfields Sports. I go swimming five days a week, from Monday to Friday. I play golf on Saturdays and I play tennis on Sundays. I really like it there!
SARA

Lots of my friends go to the park and some of them play football there. I go running there. It's great.
CHAS

I like badminton and skating. I can do both at Littleton Sports. I go swimming there on Tuesdays and Fridays because there's a nice pool, and I play football on Wednesdays.
CASSIE

37.12 DI LAS FRASES EN VOZ ALTA UTILIZANDO "GO" Y "PLAY" Y LAS FORMAS CORRECTAS DE LAS PALABRAS ENTRE PARÉNTESIS

I _go dancing_ (dance) with my friends on Mondays.

1 Milo and I _____ (cycle) in the park on Saturdays.

2 The team _____ (football) from 6pm to 7pm on Wednesdays.

3 Imelda _____ (horse ride) once a month.

4 Luther _____ (fish) during his vacation time.

5 Hannah _____ (tennis) with her cousin on Monday evenings.

---

37 ✓ CHECKLIST

⚙ "Go" y "play" ☐   Aa Deportes ☐   Hablar sobre deportes ☐

133

38.1 AFICIONES Y PASATIEMPOS

do puzzles

play cards

play chess

play board games

play computer games / play video games

read

draw

write

paint

take photos

play a musical instrument

walk / hike

cook

bake

sew

knit

watch television

watch a movie (US)
watch a film (UK)

see a play

play sport /
do exercise

go to the gym

do yoga

listen to music

go camping

go bird watching

go out for a meal

do the gardening

visit a museum /
art gallery

meet friends

go on vacation (US)
go on holiday (UK)

go sightseeing

go shopping

Los adverbios de frecuencia muestran la frecuencia con que se hace algo, desde lo que se hace muy a menudo ("always") hasta lo que no se hace nunca ("never").

⚙ **Lenguaje** Adverbios de frecuencia
Aa Vocabulario Pasatiempos
🧩 **Habilidad** Hablar sobre el tiempo libre

39.1 VOCABULARIO ADVERBIOS DE FRECUENCIA

Utiliza los adverbios de frecuencia para indicar la periodicidad con la que haces algo. Normalmente, el adverbio va entre el sujeto y el verbo.

100%
I **always** watch TV at night.

I **usually** eat dinner at 7pm.

I **often** walk to work unless it's raining.

I **sometimes** go shopping on the weekend.

0%
I **never** go to the gym. I'm too lazy!

39.2 PUNTO CLAVE ADVERBIOS DE FRECUENCIA

Las expresiones temporales suelen ir al final y se usan adverbios de frecuencia.

SUJETO	ADVERBIO DE FRECUENCIA	ACTIVIDAD	EXPRESIÓN TEMPORAL
I	always	watch TV	at night.

39.3 VUELVE A ESCRIBIR LAS FRASES PONIENDO LAS PALABRAS EN SU ORDEN CORRECTO

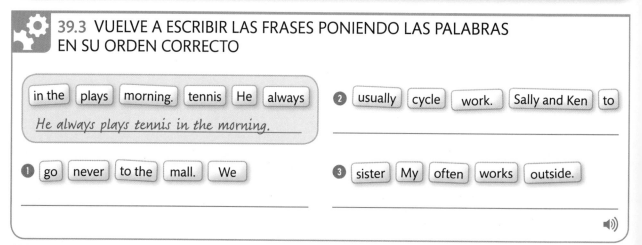

in the | plays | morning. | tennis | He | always

He always plays tennis in the morning.

② usually | cycle | work. | Sally and Ken | to
_____

① go | never | to the | mall. | We
_____

③ sister | My | often | works | outside.
_____

39.4 ESCUCHA EL AUDIO Y CONECTA EL PASATIEMPO CON SU FRECUENCIA

Ben participa en una encuesta sobre a qué dedica
su tiempo libre. Escucha sus respuestas.

always   sometimes   usually   often   usually   never

39.5 OBSERVA LA TABLA Y DI LAS FRASES EN VOZ ALTA, COMPLETANDO LOS ESPACIOS

Simon __always__ plays tennis on Fridays.
He __sometimes__ goes skiing in the winter.

1. Nico _____ swims after work.
   He _____ watches TV on the weekend.

2. Meg _____ goes surfing in Hawaii.
   She _____ dances all night.

3. Alma _____ reads on vacation.
   She _____ plays golf on Sundays.

4. Carrie _____ goes to bed late and
   she _____ eats breakfast.

39.6 CÓMO FUNCIONA PREGUNTAS SOBRE EL TIEMPO LIBRE

Utiliza diferentes frases para preguntar sobre la frecuencia con que alguien hace una actividad y cuándo se lleva a cabo dicha actividad en concreto.

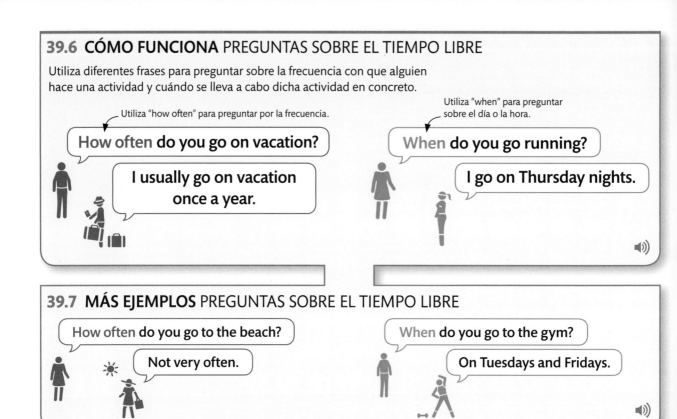

39.7 MÁS EJEMPLOS PREGUNTAS SOBRE EL TIEMPO LIBRE

39.8 MARCA LA PREGUNTA CORRECTA PARA CADA RESPUESTA

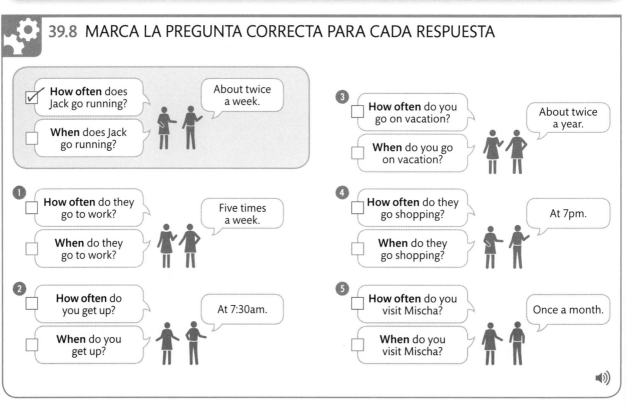

39.9 ESCRIBE UNA PREGUNTA BASADA EN CADA AFIRMACIÓN UTILIZANDO "HOW OFTEN" Y "WHEN"

She goes dancing twice a week.
How often does she go dancing?

1 They visit their grandparents on Saturdays.

_____

2 We go skating during the winter.

_____

3 He usually plays hockey three times a month.

_____

4 You go shopping on Fridays.

_____

5 They see their parents every weekend.

_____

6 He never walks the dog.

_____

7 We sometimes go skating on the lake.

_____

🔊

39.10 HAZ PREGUNTAS EN VOZ ALTA BASADAS EN LAS AFIRMACIONES

How often do you listen to music?

I listen to music every night.

1 _____

I do yoga on Monday nights.

2 _____

I sometimes go to the movies.

3 _____

I go skateboarding three times a month.

4 _____

I arrive at work at 8am.

5 _____

I usually go surfing once a week.

🔊

39 ✓ CHECKLIST

⚙ Adverbios de frecuencia ☐   **Aa** Pasatiempos ☐   👤 Hablar sobre el tiempo libre ☐

40 Qué nos gusta y qué no

Verbos como "love", "like" y "hate" expresan tus sentimientos hacia algo. Puedes utilizarlos con sustantivos o gerundios.

🔧 **Lenguaje** "Love", "like" y "hate"
Aa Vocabulario Comida, deportes y pasatiempos
🧩 **Habilidad** Hablar sobre tus gustos

40.1 PUNTO CLAVE NUESTROS GUSTOS CON SUSTANTIVOS

Puedes utilizar estos verbos para hablar sobre los sustantivos.

Utiliza "do not" o "don't", y "does not" o "doesn't" para hacer frases negativas.

She likes tennis.

Max doesn't like pizza.

I love chocolate.

Esto significa que realmente te gusta.

They hate coffee.

Esto es más negativo que "don't like".

> **NOTA**
> "Don't like" y "dislike" significan lo mismo, pero se usa más "don't like" en inglés oral.

40.2 MÁS EJEMPLOS NUESTROS GUSTOS CON SUSTANTIVOS

I love fries.

You don't like baseball.

The cat doesn't like its food.

Oliver hates board games.

40.3 CONECTA CADA IMAGEN CON LA FRASE QUE LE CORRESPONDE

Shania hates mice.

Sam doesn't like TV.

Ava and Elsa love the mountains.

Cats don't like the rain.

Manuel likes his book.

40.4 ESCRIBE LA FORMA NEGATIVA DE CADA FRASE UTILIZANDO "DOESN'T" O "DON'T"

Jack likes London. | *Jack doesn't like London.*

1. Imelda hates pasta.
2. My dog loves steak.
3. Our grandfather likes coffee.
4. I love the sea.
5. Sam and Jen hate hockey.
6. You like the countryside.
7. We like our new cell phones.

40.5 ESCUCHA EL AUDIO Y MARCA LAS RESPUESTAS CORRECTAS

Anna habla en la radio sobre lo que le gusta y lo que le desagrada.

Anna likes Matt's...
hat ☐   glasses. ☑

1. She doesn't like...
hockey ☐   golf. ☐

2. Anna likes...
some actors ☐   all actors. ☐

3. She loves...
pizza ☐   pasta. ☐

4. She doesn't like...
spiders ☐   snakes. ☐

40.6 USA EL DIAGRAMA PARA CREAR NUEVE FRASES CORRECTAS Y DILAS EN VOZ ALTA

I love cats.

| I / You / Milly | love / hates | cats. / curry. / this house. |

Empieza con un nombre o un pronombre.

Elige un verbo.

Termina la frase con un sustantivo.

141

40.7 PUNTO CLAVE NUESTROS GUSTOS CON GERUNDIOS

Puedes utilizar verbos como "like" y "hate"
con un gerundio para hablar de actividades.

They like **playing chess.**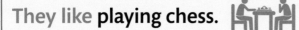

Ed doesn't like **cycling.**

I love **swimming.**

She hates **shopping.**

40.8 MÁS EJEMPLOS NUESTROS GUSTOS CON GERUNDIOS

Vi and Lu love **playing golf.**

I don't like **working late.**

Elliot loves **watching birds.**

You like **drinking coffee.**

40.9 ESCUCHA EL AUDIO Y CONECTA CADA PERSONA CON LA ACTIVIDAD QUE LE GUSTA O LE DESAGRADA

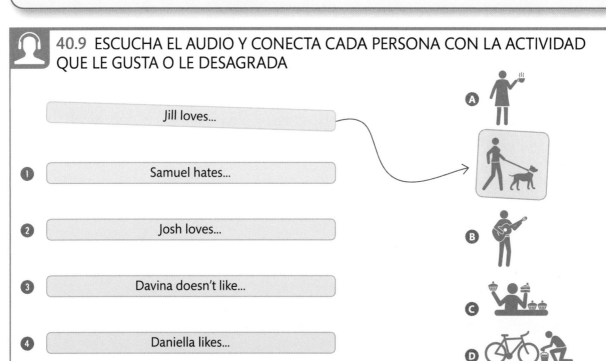

Jill loves...

1 Samuel hates...

2 Josh loves...

3 Davina doesn't like...

4 Daniella likes...

A

B

C

D

48 OLDTON NEWS

CLUBS AND SOCIETIES

An Oldton student tells us about some local clubs

I am Mark Watson and I'm at Oldton University. This is the first week of classes and students are trying lots of activities. This is what I think of them…

Chocolate Club: Do you like chocolate? Well, the people in this club love it! I don't like chocolate, so this club is not for me. They make chocolate cakes and chocolate drinks.

Dancing Club: My girlfriend loves this club. She goes twice a week. It is great exercise, but I hate it because I am very clumsy.

Computer Gaming Club: I love playing computer games at home. I really like playing with other people, too, so I like this club. There are lots of players there every week.

Chess Club: I love playing chess. I go to this club because it's a lot of fun. The players are very good, so I don't win very often. It makes me a better player.

Skateboarding Club: This is a fantastic club where you can learn from great skateboarders. This club meets three times a week and it's a great place to make new friends. I love it!

Mark loves chocolate.
True ☐ **False** ☑

① People make cakes at Chocolate Club.
True ☐ **False** ☐

② Mark's girlfriend hates dancing.
True ☐ **False** ☐

③ Mark likes dancing.
True ☐ **False** ☐

④ He loves computer games.
True ☐ **False** ☐

⑤ He doesn't like the chess club.
True ☐ **False** ☐

⑥ The players are very good.
True ☐ **False** ☐

⑦ Skateboarding Club is horrible.
True ☐ **False** ☐

⑧ Skateboarding Club meets three times a week.
True ☐ **False** ☐

⑨ Mark loves three of the clubs.
True ☐ **False** ☐

40.11 VOCABULARIO RAZONES PARA QUE ALGO NOS GUSTE O NOS DESAGRADE

Puedes usar estos adjetivos para decir por qué te gusta o desagrada algo.

exciting

interesting

tiring

fun

delicious

disgusting

boring

40.12 PUNTO CLAVE PREGUNTAS SOBRE GUSTOS CON "DO"

Utiliza "do" o "does" para preguntar si a alguien le gusta algo.

Utiliza "do" para hacer una pregunta.

Do you like chocolate?

Puedes usar "it" para evitar repetir el sujeto.

Yes, I do. It's delicious.

Do you like fishing?

No, I don't. It's boring.

40.13 PUNTO CLAVE PREGUNTAS SOBRE GUSTOS CON "WHY"

Puedes utilizar "why" para averiguar las razones por las que a alguien le gusta o le desagrada algo.

Utiliza "why" para preguntar por la razón.

Why do you like basketball?

Puedes utilizar "because" para unir las dos partes de tu respuesta.

I love it because it's exciting.

Why don't you like skating?

I hate it because it's tiring.

40.14 HAZ PREGUNTAS EN FUNCIÓN DE LAS AFIRMACIONES

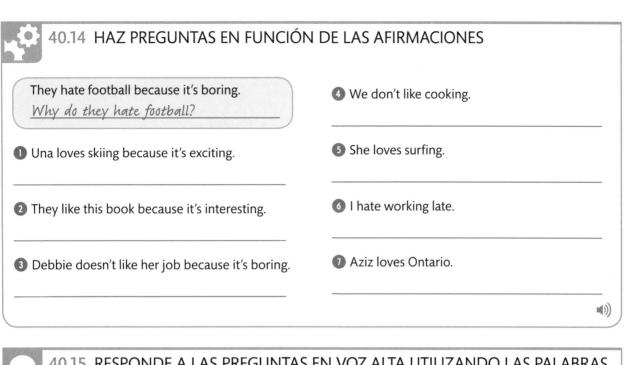

They hate football because it's boring.
Why do they hate football?

❶ Una loves skiing because it's exciting.

_____

❷ They like this book because it's interesting.

_____

❸ Debbie doesn't like her job because it's boring.

_____

❹ We don't like cooking.

_____

❺ She loves surfing.

_____

❻ I hate working late.

_____

❼ Aziz loves Ontario.

_____

40.15 RESPONDE A LAS PREGUNTAS EN VOZ ALTA UTILIZANDO LAS PALABRAS DEL RECUADRO

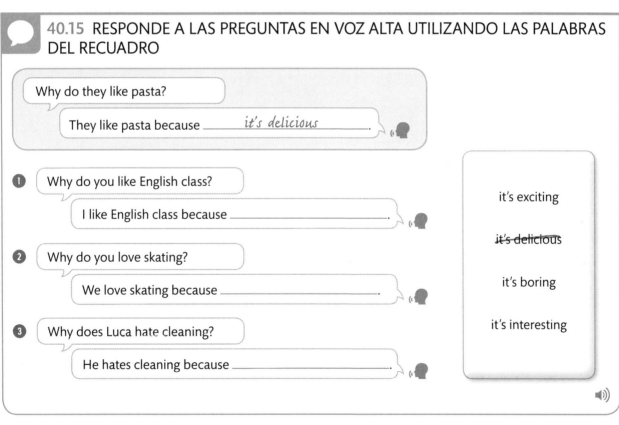

Why do they like pasta?

They like pasta because *it's delicious*.

❶ Why do you like English class?

I like English class because _____.

❷ Why do you love skating?

We love skating because _____.

❸ Why does Luca hate cleaning?

He hates cleaning because _____.

it's exciting

~~it's delicious~~

it's boring

it's interesting

---

40 ✔ CHECKLIST

✿ "Love", "like" y "hate" ☐   **Aa** Comida, deportes y pasatiempos ☐   🧩 Hablar sobre tus gustos ☐

41.1 MÚSICA

classical music

hip-hop

jazz

country

opera

soul

rap

rock

pop

Latin

orchestra

band /group

play the trumpet

guitar player

concert

festival

sing a song

singer

headphones

album

dance

microphone

conductor

audience

41.2 INSTRUMENTOS MUSICALES

guitar

electric guitar

piano

keyboard

violin

saxophone

harmonica

trumpet

drum

flute

42 Expresar preferencias

Utiliza "like" y "love" para indicar cuánto te diviertes con algo. "Favorite" se utiliza para identificar las cosas que más te gustan.

⚙ **Lenguaje** Utilizar "favorite"
Aa Vocabulario Comida y música
🧩 **Habilidad** Hablar sobre tus cosas favoritas

42.1 PUNTO CLAVE UTILIZAR "FAVORITE"

"Like" y "love" son verbos, de modo que necesitan sujetos y objetos. "Favorite" es un adjetivo y siempre va junto a un sustantivo o gerundio.

Recuerda, este verbo es más fuerte que "like".

I like jazz and I love soul, but my favorite type of music is rock.

★★★

Esta palabra indica que esto es lo que más te gusta.

"Favorite" puede ir seguido de un sustantivo o por la frase "type of" y un sustantivo.

42.2 MÁS EJEMPLOS UTILIZAR "FAVORITE"

"Italian" es un tipo de comida, no un plato en particular.

She likes salsa dancing.

Abdul loves sailing.

Her favorite type of food is Italian.

Basketball is his favourite sport.

Así se escribe en inglés británico.

42.3 ESCUCHA EL AUDIO Y RESPONDE A LAS PREGUNTAS

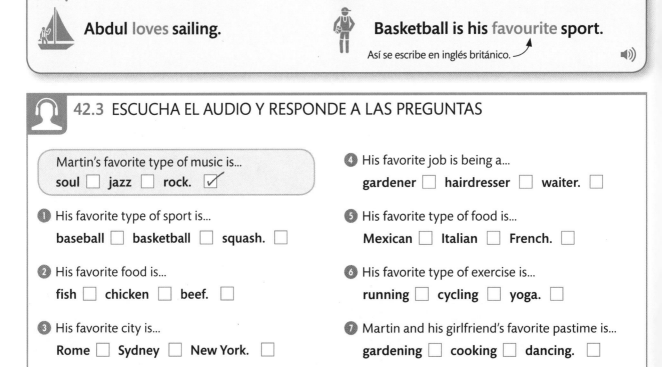

Martin's favorite type of music is...
soul ☐ **jazz** ☐ **rock.** ☑

① His favorite type of sport is...
baseball ☐ **basketball** ☐ **squash.** ☐

② His favorite food is...
fish ☐ **chicken** ☐ **beef.** ☐

③ His favorite city is...
Rome ☐ **Sydney** ☐ **New York.** ☐

④ His favorite job is being a...
gardener ☐ **hairdresser** ☐ **waiter.** ☐

⑤ His favorite type of food is...
Mexican ☐ **Italian** ☐ **French.** ☐

⑥ His favorite type of exercise is...
running ☐ **cycling** ☐ **yoga.** ☐

⑦ Martin and his girlfriend's favorite pastime is...
gardening ☐ **cooking** ☐ **dancing.** ☐

Aa 42.4 MARCA EL DIBUJO QUE CORRESPONDE A CADA FRASE

Jack's **favorite** music is jazz.

A ☐ B ☑ C ☐

❸ Aman's **favorite** sport is hockey.

A ☐ B ☐ C ☐

❶ Ava's **favorite** thing is her new dress.

A ☐ B ☐ C ☐

❹ Mo and Jamie's **favorite** food is chocolate.

A ☐ B ☐ C ☐

❷ Deborah's **favorite** pet is her dog.

A ☐ B ☐ C ☐

❺ Atif's **favorite** city is New York.

A ☐ B ☐ C ☐

Aa 42.5 COMPLETA LOS ESPACIOS CON LAS PALABRAS DEL RECUADRO

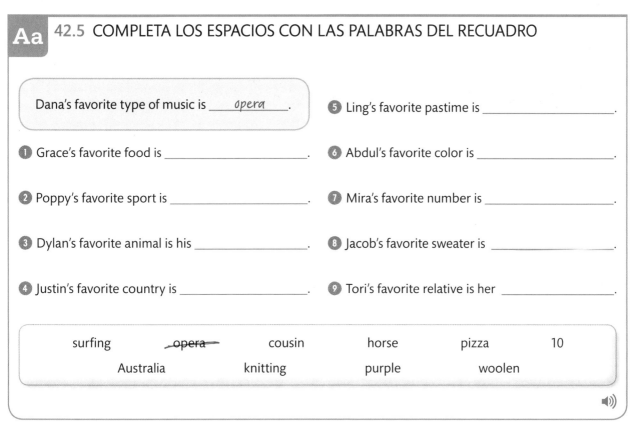

Dana's favorite type of music is ___opera___.

❶ Grace's favorite food is _____.

❷ Poppy's favorite sport is _____.

❸ Dylan's favorite animal is his _____.

❹ Justin's favorite country is _____.

❺ Ling's favorite pastime is _____.

❻ Abdul's favorite color is _____.

❼ Mira's favorite number is _____.

❽ Jacob's favorite sweater is _____.

❾ Tori's favorite relative is her _____.

| surfing | ~~opera~~ | cousin | horse | pizza | 10 |
| Australia | | knitting | purple | woolen | |

42.6 OBSERVA ESTOS PERFILES ONLINE Y COMPLETA LOS ESPACIOS. LUEGO DI LAS FRASES EN VOZ ALTA

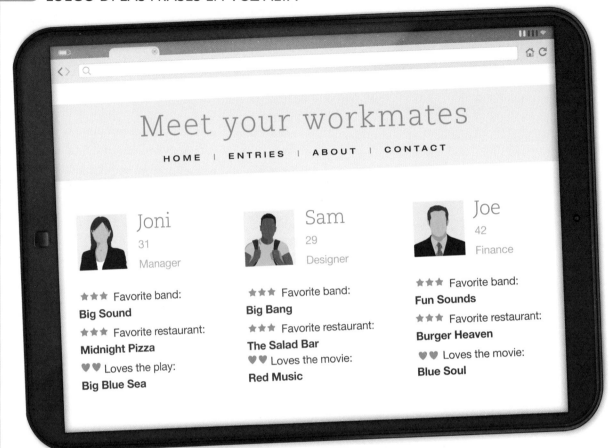

Meet your workmates

HOME | ENTRIES | ABOUT | CONTACT

Joni
31
Manager

★★★ Favorite band:
Big Sound
★★★ Favorite restaurant:
Midnight Pizza
♥♥ Loves the play:
Big Blue Sea

Sam
29
Designer

★★★ Favorite band:
Big Bang
★★★ Favorite restaurant:
The Salad Bar
♥♥ Loves the movie:
Red Music

Joe
42
Finance

★★★ Favorite band:
Fun Sounds
★★★ Favorite restaurant:
Burger Heaven
♥♥ Loves the movie:
Blue Soul

Joni's favorite band is ___Big Sound___.

④ Sam's favorite restaurant is _____.

① Sam's _____ is Big Bang.

⑤ Joe's _____ is Burger Heaven.

② Joe's favorite band is _____.

⑥ Joni _____ called Big Blue Sea.

③ Joni's _____ is Midnight Pizza.

⑦ Joe loves the movie called _____.

42.7 LEE EL ARTÍCULO Y RESPONDE A LAS PREGUNTAS

What is the favorite time to exercise?
morning ☑ afternoon ☐ evening ☐

1 What type of exercise is their favorite?

yoga ☐ running ☐ swimming ☐

2 What is Stanton people's favorite type of food?

pizza ☐ burgers ☐ ice cream ☐

3 What is their favorite sport?

golf ☐ football ☐ surfing ☐

4 Their favorite night out is going to...

the movies ☐ the theater ☐ a restaurant. ☐

Town favorites

What's your favorite time to exercise? The morning, the afternoon, or the evening? In Stanton, people say it's the morning because there are too many other things to do in the evening. The favorite exercise is yoga: 20 classes take place each week.

Stanton townspeople like food. They eat lots of it: 4,000,000 burgers, 2,000,000 pizzas, and 3,000,000 ice cream cones every year.

And how about sports? In Stanton, there are hundreds of golfers and football players, but the favorite sport is surfing.

People like going out in the evening. Many love movies and the theater, but that's not their favorite night out. It's dinner in a restaurant. Food again. That's not a surprise!

---

42 ✓ CHECKLIST

⚙ Utilizar "favorite" ☐   **Aa** Comida y música ☐   🧩 Hablar sobre tus cosas favoritas ☐

↻ REPASA LO QUE HAS APRENDIDO EN LAS UNIDADES 36–42

NUEVO LENGUAJE	FRASES DE EJEMPLO	☑	UNIDAD
"GO" CON GERUNDIOS	I go swimming **on Mondays** and I play tennis **with my brother on Fridays.**	☐	37.1, 37.7
ADVERBIOS DE FRECUENCIA	I always watch TV **at night,** and I sometimes go the the movies.	☐	39.1
PREGUNTAS SOBRE EL TIEMPO LIBRE	How often do you **go on vacation?** When does she **go running?**	☐	39.6
QUÉ NOS GUSTA Y QUÉ NO	She likes **tennis.** Max doesn't like **pizza.** I love **swimming.** She hates **shopping.**	☐	40.1, 40.7
PREGUNTAS SOBRE GUSTOS	Do you like **chocolate?** Why do you like **basketball?**	☐	40.12, 40.13
UTILIZAR "FAVORITE"	My favorite type of **music is rock.**	☐	42.1

43.1 HABILIDADES

jump

climb

fly

ride

drive

play

kick

throw

hit

catch

see

listen

whisper

talk

speak

shout

carry

make (a snowman)

do (homework)

think

act

remember

understand

spell

sit

stand up

walk

move

lift

work

add

subtract

44 Qué sabes hacer y qué no

Utiliza "can" para hablar de las cosas que sabes hacer,
como por ejemplo ir en bicicleta o tocar la guitarra.
Utiliza "cannot" o "can't" para cosas que no sabes hacer.

🔧 **Lenguaje** "Can", "can't" y "cannot"
Aa Vocabulario Talentos y habilidades
🧩 **Habilidad** Expresar qué sabes hacer y qué no

44.1 PUNTO CLAVE "CAN / CANNOT / CAN'T"

"Can" se coloca entre el
sujeto y el verbo. Después
de "can" el verbo cambia
a su forma base (infinitivo
sin "to").

NOTA
La forma larga
negativa "cannot" se
escribe siempre como
una palabra, no como
dos separadas.

I can ride a bicycle.
Forma base del verbo.

He can play the guitar.
"Can" es invariable, y
no cambia con el sujeto.

I { cannot / can't } sing jazz songs.
Forma contraída de "cannot".

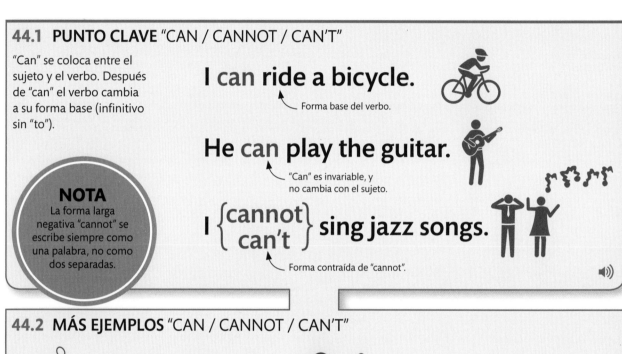

44.2 MÁS EJEMPLOS "CAN / CANNOT / CAN'T"

 Janet can play tennis.

 He cannot climb the tree.

 Bob can swim well.

 They can't lift the box.

44.3 CÓMO FUNCIONA "CAN / CANNOT / CAN'T"

SUJETO	"CAN / CANNOT / CAN'T"	FORMA BASE	OBJETO
She	can cannot can't	ride	a bicycle.

44.4 VUELVE A ESCRIBIR LAS FRASES CORRIGIENDO LOS ERRORES

| carry | chair. | can | Sylvia | the |

Sylvia can carry the chair.

3 | tonight. | in the | They | tent | can | sleep |

_____

1 | ride | Paul | a | bicycle. | cannot |

_____

4 | the | hill. | cannot | up | I | walk |

_____

2 | come | cannot | Manuel | party. | to the |

_____

5 | can | carry | I | this | car. | to the | box |

_____

44.5 TACHA LA PALABRA INCORRECTA DE CADA FRASE

My son is sick. He ~~can~~ / can't go to school today.

1 Jo's pen doesn't work. She can / **can't** write her letter.

2 I understand the homework, so I **can** / can't do it.

3 The museum is closed. We can / **can't** get in.

4 I have the car today, so I **can** / can't drive you.

5 It's cold outside, so we can / **can't** have a picnic.

6 Tony needs to work late, so he can / **can't** come.

7 We can / **can't** play tennis. It's too dark.

44.6 COMPLETA LOS ESPACIOS Y ESCRIBE CADA FRASE DE TRES MANERAS DISTINTAS

I can read Russian.	I cannot read Russian.	I can't read Russian.
1 _____	Shirley cannot drive a car.	_____
2 Ben and Julie can carry boxes.	_____	_____
3 _____	_____	Ilaria can't spell English words.
4 _____	He cannot go to work.	_____

155

44.7 PUNTO CLAVE PREGUNTAS Y RESPUESTAS CORTAS

Para hacer una pregunta con "can", coloca "can" antes del sujeto. Cuando respondes preguntas formuladas con "can", no es necesario repetir todas las palabras de la pregunta.

Can you **ride a bicycle?**

Yes, I can.

No, I can't.

44.8 MÁS EJEMPLOS PREGUNTAS Y RESPUESTAS CORTAS

Can she **speak Japanese?**

Yes, she can.

Can we **climb that mountain?**

No, we can't.

Can they **swim?**

No, they can't.

Can you **move that chair?**

Yes, I can.

44.9 DI LAS FRASES EN VOZ ALTA, COMPLETANDO LOS ESPACIOS

Can you lift that heavy box?

Yes, _I can._

4 Can you spell "excited?"

Yes, _____

1 Can he play the piano?

No, _____

5 Can we lift this big table?

No, _____

2 Can they catch that big fish?

Yes, _____

6 Can she fly a kite in this weather?

Yes, _____

3 Can you hit that ball over there?

No, _____

7 Can they cycle into town?

No, _____

44.10 ESCRIBE LA PREGUNTA PARA CADA RESPUESTA

> Paul and Mary can speak Chinese.
> *Can Paul and Mary speak Chinese?*

1 The dog can jump over the wall.

_____

2 Denise can touch her toes.

_____

3 I can lift my son onto my shoulders.

_____

4 Grandma can see the TV.

_____

5 I can hit the tennis ball over the net.

_____

🔊

44.11 ESCUCHA EL AUDIO Y RESPONDE A LAS PREGUNTAS

Sheila y Mark hablan de las cosas que no saben cocinar.

> Sheila can make a salad.
> **True** ✓ **False** ☐

1 Sheila doesn't eat meat.
True ☐ **False** ☐

2 Mark can't cook a roast chicken.
True ☐ **False** ☐

3 Sheila and Mark can both cook vegetables.
True ☐ **False** ☐

4 Sheila can make an apple pie.
True ☐ **False** ☐

44.12 COMPLETA LOS ESPACIOS CON "CAN" O "CANNOT"

> Janet is a chef. She _____ *can* _____ cook very well.

1 Paul and Jerry don't like the ocean because they _____ swim.

2 I ride my bike to work because I _____ drive.

3 Jim cannot climb over the wall, but he _____ walk around it.

4 My mother _____ lift that bag because it's too heavy.

5 My sister Penny loves music and _____ dance to any song.

🔊

44 ✓ CHECKLIST

⚙ "Can", "can't" y "cannot" ☐   **Aa** Talentos y habilidades ☐   🧩 Expresar qué sabes hacer y qué no ☐

45 Describir acciones

Las palabras como "quietly" y "loudly" se llaman adverbios. Proporcionan más información sobre los verbos. Se utilizan para describir cómo se hace algo.

⚙ **Lenguaje** Adverbios regulares e irregulares
Aa Vocabulario Aficiones y actividades
🧩 **Habilidad** Describir actividades

45.1 PUNTO CLAVE UTILIZAR ADVERBIOS

Normalmente, los adverbios se colocan después del verbo que describen.

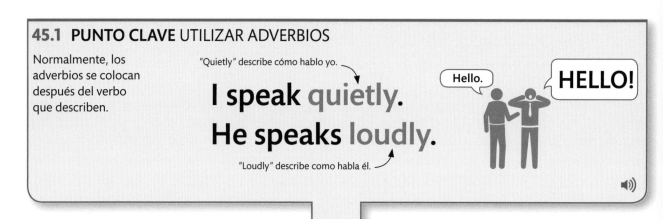

"Quietly" describe cómo hablo yo.

I speak quietly.

He speaks loudly.

"Loudly" describe como habla él.

Hello.

HELLO!

45.2 MÁS EJEMPLOS UTILIZAR ADVERBIOS

 A tortoise moves slowly.

 She sings beautifully.

Horses can run quickly.

I can play the piano badly.

45.3 COMPLETA LOS ESPACIOS CON LAS PALABRAS DEL RECUADRO

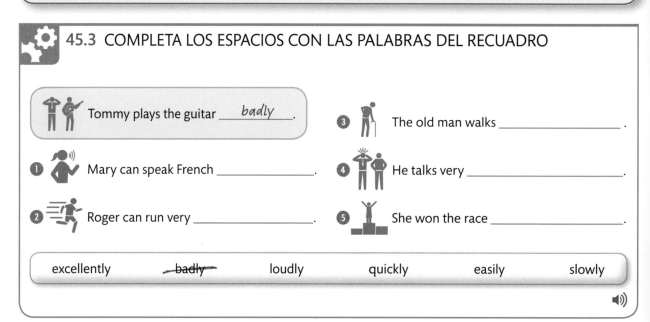

Tommy plays the guitar _____badly_____.

① Mary can speak French _____.

② Roger can run very _____.

③ The old man walks _____.

④ He talks very _____.

⑤ She won the race _____.

| excellently | ~~badly~~ | loudly | quickly | easily | slowly |

45.4 PUNTO CLAVE ADVERBIOS REGULARES E IRREGULARES

ADVERBIOS REGULARES

Para formar la mayoría de los adverbios, añade "ly" a los adjetivos. Si el adjetivo termina en "y", suprime la "y" y añade "ily" para formar el adverbio.

bad → badly

careful → carefully

easy → easily

Quita la "y" y añade "ily".

ADVERBIOS IRREGULARES

Mientras que algunos adverbios son totalmente diferentes de los adjetivos, otros, en cambio, son idénticos. Los últimos son los adverbios irregulares.

good → well

El adverbio es totalmente diferente del adjetivo.

hard → hard

El adverbio es igual que el adjetivo.

early → early

Los adjetivos terminados en "ly" no cambian al convertirse en adverbios.

Aa 45.5 BUSCA 8 ADVERBIOS Y ESCRÍBELOS EN SU COLUMNA

```
E A S I L Y W L K Q G
B N O Y U T E O A U R
A J S L O X L S G I W
D F L O U D L Y T C E
L F H A B L W H F K M
Y A G A R U E A R L Y
C S F U S Y Q R V Y W
I T R S L K A D B M S
```

REGULAR

1. Loudly
2. _____
3. _____
4. _____

IRREGULAR

5. Fast
6. _____
7. _____
8. _____

⚙ 45.6 VUELVE A ESCRIBIR LAS FRASES CORRIGIENDO LOS ERRORES

My friend John walks very quick.
My friend John walks very quickly.

1. You speak English very good.

_____

2. Damian cooks burgers bad.

_____

3. I can get to your house easy.

_____

4. Benjy always listens careful.

_____

5. My brother always works hardly.

_____

6. Sammy always plays his guitar loud.

_____

45.7 OTRAS FORMAS SOY BUENO EN ALGO

Si eres "good at" en algo, es que lo haces bien. Utiliza un gerundio o un sustantivo relacionado con la actividad que haces y colócalo después de la frase para expresar que eres "good at".

She can run well.

⬇

She's good at running.

Utiliza el gerundio después de "good at".

45.8 CÓMO FUNCIONA "GOOD AT / BAD AT"

La forma negativa de "good at" es "bad at".

SUJETO + VERBO	"GOOD AT / BAD AT"	GERUNDIO / SUSTANTIVO
She's	good at bad at	skiing. English.

45.9 MÁS EJEMPLOS "GOOD AT / BAD AT"

 Aziz is good at climbing **trees.**

I am bad at making **cakes.**

 Kate is good at soccer.

Harris is bad at chess.

45.10 VUELVE A ESCRIBIR LAS FRASES PONIENDO LAS PALABRAS EN SU ORDEN CORRECTO

the guitar. | good at | playing | Pablo is

Pablo is good at playing the guitar.

1. is | at | good | My horse | jumping.

_____

2. bad at | early. | getting up | I am

_____

3. writing | Mary is | bad at | German.

_____

4. good | swimming. | at | are | Jo and Bob

_____

5. cleaning. | is | Millie | bad at

_____

45.11 VUELVE A ESCRIBIR CADA FRASE EN SU OTRA FORMA

She can play the piano well.
She's good at playing the piano.

1 Conchita can play basketball well.

_____

2 You're good at driving a van.

_____

3 Shania and Dave can surf well.

_____

4 My father is bad at speaking English.

_____

5 Manu can't write stories well.

_____

🔊

45.12 ESCUCHA EL AUDIO Y MARCA QUIÉN ES BUENO O MALO EN CADA ACTIVIDAD

Good at ✔ Bad at ☐

1 Good at ☐ Bad at ☐

2 Good at ☐ Bad at ☐

3 Good at ☐ Bad at ☐

4 Good at ☐ Bad at ☐

45.13 USA EL DIAGRAMA PARA CREAR 12 FRASES CORRECTAS Y DILAS EN VOZ ALTA

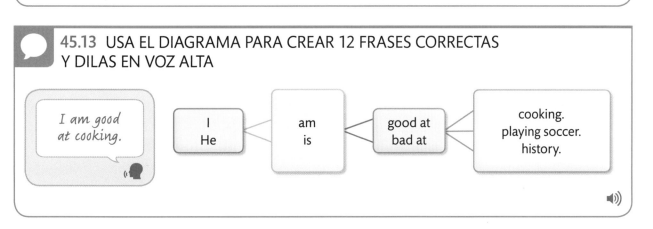

I am good at cooking.

| I / He | am / is | good at / bad at | cooking. / playing soccer. / history. |

🔊

46 Describir habilidades

Palabras como "quite" y "very" son adverbios modificadores. Puedes utilizarlos antes de otros adverbios para dar más información sobre cómo haces algo.

🔧 **Lenguaje** Adverbios modificadores
Aa Vocabulario Aptitudes y habilidades
🧩 **Habilidad** Decir lo bien que haces algo

46.1 PUNTO CLAVE ADVERBIOS MODIFICADORES

Si haces algo "quite well", eres bueno haciéndolo pero no muy bueno. Si lo haces "very" o "really well", eres muy bueno.

"Quite" modifica el adverbio principal "well", y se coloca antes.

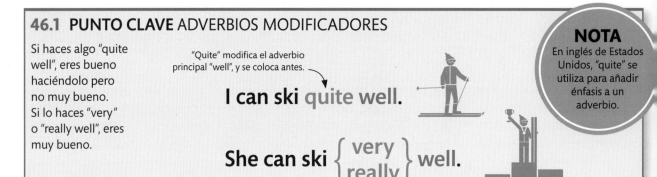

I can ski **quite** well.

She can ski { **very** / **really** } well.

NOTA
En inglés de Estados Unidos, "quite" se utiliza para añadir énfasis a un adverbio.

46.2 MÁS EJEMPLOS ADVERBIOS MODIFICADORES

 Ben can climb **really** high.

 My dad dances **quite** well.

 Jenny can swim **very** well.

 I speak Spanish **quite** well.

Aa 46.3 CONECTA EL COMIENZO Y EL FINAL DE CADA FRASE

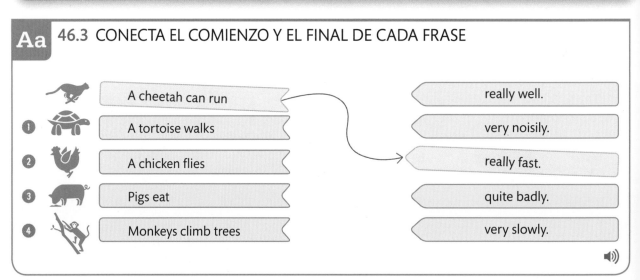

A cheetah can run — really fast.

① A tortoise walks — really well.

② A chicken flies — very noisily.

③ Pigs eat — quite badly.

④ Monkeys climb trees — very slowly.

46.4 PUNTO CLAVE ADVERBIOS MODIFICADORES CON "GOOD AT"

También puedes utilizar los adverbios modificadores con las expresiones "good at" y "bad at".

She can play golf quite well.

She's quite good at **playing golf.**

"Quite" modifica a "good at".

Recuerda que después de "good at" y "bad at" va un gerundio.

You can play golf { very / really } **well.**

You're { very / really } good at **playing golf.**

"Very / really" van antes de "good at".

46.5 LEE EL INFORME Y RESPONDE A LAS PREGUNTAS

English report: Juan Ramirez

How good is Juan at learning vocabulary?
Quite good ☑   **Really good** ☐

① How good is he at speaking English?
Quite good ☐   **Really good** ☐

② How good is Juan at reading?
Quite good ☐   **Really good** ☐

③ How good is he at listening to English?
Quite good ☐   **Really good** ☐

④ How good is Juan at writing English?
Quite good ☐   **Really good** ☐

Writing 99%	Excellent.
Vocabulary 65%	Ok, but you need to study more.
Speaking 95%	Well done.
Listening 66%	Better. Try watching more English movies to improve.
Reading 63%	Ok. You need to read more English texts to improve.

---

46 ⊘ CHECKLIST

⚙ Adverbios modificadores ☐   **Aa** Aptitudes y habilidades ☐   🧩 Decir lo bien que haces algo ☐

47 Deseos y ambiciones

Puedes utilizar "I want" y "I would like" para hablar de lo que quieres hacer. También puedes usar la forma negativa de estas frases para indicar lo que no te gustaría hacer.

⚙ **Lenguaje** "Would" y "want"
Aa Vocabulario Actividades de ocio
🧩 **Habilidad** Hablar de tus ambiciones

47.1 PUNTO CLAVE "I WOULD LIKE / I WANT"

"I would like" es similar a "I want", pero "I want" es más directo, tiene mayor intensidad.

He wants to write a book.

Tiene un mayor deseo de hacer algo.

I would like to climb a mountain.

I'd like to go scuba diving.

Esta es la forma contraída de "I would".

47.2 CÓMO FUNCIONA "I WOULD LIKE / I'D LIKE"

"Would" es un verbo modal, por lo que su forma no cambia.

SUJETO	VERBO MODAL	VERBO	INFINITIVO + OBJETO
I / You / He / She	would	like	to go cycling.
We / You / They			

47.3 MÁS EJEMPLOS "I'D LIKE / I WANT"

She'd like to go to Bali.

We'd like to cook dinner.

I'd like to drive a sports car.

He wants to go surfing in Hawaii.

We want to go on a boat.

The dog wants to jump in the river.

47.4 COMPLETA LOS ESPACIOS Y ESCRIBE CADA FRASE DE TRES MANERAS DISTINTAS

I want to buy a house.	I would like to buy a house.	I'd like to buy a house.
❶		He'd like to get a dog.
❷	You would like to work in Turkey.	
❸ We want to learn Chinese.		
❹		They'd like to start a rock band.

Aa 47.5 CONECTA LOS DIBUJOS CON LAS DESCRIPCIONES

| He'd like to travel around Asia. | He'd like to act in a musical. | He wants to be in the Olympics. | She wants to work with lions in Africa. | She'd like to sail a boat. |

47.6 USA EL DIAGRAMA PARA CREAR 12 FRASES CORRECTAS Y DILAS EN VOZ ALTA

I'd like to climb this tree.

| I'd like / I want / She wants | to climb / to read | this tree. / that mountain. / a newspaper. / another book. |

47.7 PUNTO CLAVE LA FORMA NEGATIVA DE "I WOULD LIKE / I WANT"

Utiliza "not" después de "would" para construir la forma negativa. "Don't" y "doesn't" se colocan antes de "want".

I would not like to go snowboarding.

I wouldn't like to go shopping.

↳ La forma contraída de "would not".

They don't want to go fishing.

↳ "Don't" va antes de "want".

47.8 MÁS EJEMPLOS LA FORMA NEGATIVA DE "I WOULD LIKE / I WANT"

They wouldn't like **to go swimming.**   We don't want **to eat dinner.**

She wouldn't like **to be a hairdresser.**   He doesn't want **to go shopping.**

47.9 COMPLETA LOS ESPACIOS Y ESCRIBE CADA FRASE DE TRES MANERAS DISTINTAS

I would not like to go skiing.	I wouldn't like to go skiing.	I don't want to go skiing.
① _____	_____	He doesn't want to play tennis.
② _____	She wouldn't like to study science.	_____
③ _____	_____	They don't want to go to work.
④ You would not like to sing.	_____	_____
⑤ _____	We wouldn't like to go diving.	_____

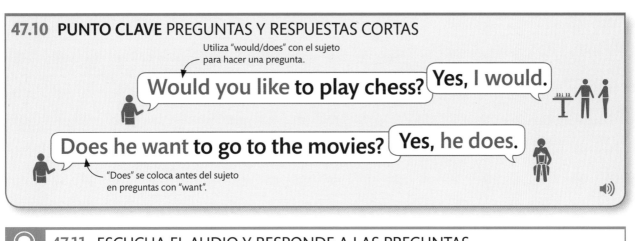

47.10 PUNTO CLAVE PREGUNTAS Y RESPUESTAS CORTAS

Utiliza "would/does" con el sujeto para hacer una pregunta.

Would you like to play chess? Yes, I would.

Does he want to go to the movies? Yes, he does.

"Does" se coloca antes del sujeto en preguntas con "want".

47.11 ESCUCHA EL AUDIO Y RESPONDE A LAS PREGUNTAS

Does Mark want to play tennis later?
Yes, he does. ✓ **No, he doesn't.** ☐

③ Would Lee like to work on Saturday?
Yes, he would. ☐ **No, he wouldn't.** ☐

① Would Sarah like to go to a restaurant today?
Yes, she would. ☐ **No, she wouldn't.** ☐

④ Does Mary want to skateboard tonight?
Yes, she does. ☐ **No, she doesn't.** ☐

② Does Vangelis want to make the dinner?
Yes, he does. ☐ **No, he doesn't.** ☐

⑤ Would Anoushka like to go bowling?
Yes, she would. ☐ **No, she wouldn't.** ☐

47.12 VUELVE A ESCRIBIR LAS FRASES CORRIGIENDO LOS ERRORES

Would you **want** to go home?
Would you like to go home?

③ They **doesn't** want to go to work today.
_____

① He **don't** want to climb that hill.
_____

④ She would **want** to play tennis tonight.
_____

② I wouldn't **likes** to be a judge.
_____

⑤ I **wants** to climb that tree.
_____

48 Estudiar

Cuando hablamos de nuestros estudios, podemos utilizar "I would" y "I want" para decir qué materias te gustaría estudiar. Utiliza adverbios para decir cuánto te gustaría estudiarlas.

⚙️ **Lenguaje** Adverbios y artículos
Aa Vocabulario Asignaturas
🧩 **Habilidad** Hablar sobre tus estudios

48.1 VOCABULARIO ASIGNATURAS

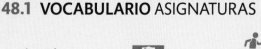
art and design

drama

physical education

English

music

math (US) maths (UK)

science

chemistry

biology

physics

geography

history

🔊

48.2 PUNTO CLAVE "REALLY / QUITE"

El adverbio "really" significa que realmente quieres hacer algo. "Quite" es menos intenso.

I love music. I'd really like to study it next term.

└ Tienes un gran deseo de hacer esto.

I like biology. I'd quite like to study it next year.

└ Tu deseo no es tan fuerte.

🔊

48.3 MÁS EJEMPLOS "REALLY / QUITE"

Bella is good at science, and she'd really like to study it at college.

Richard loves jazz, so he'd really like to go to that music festival.

This band is OK. I'd quite like to listen to their new CD.

🔊

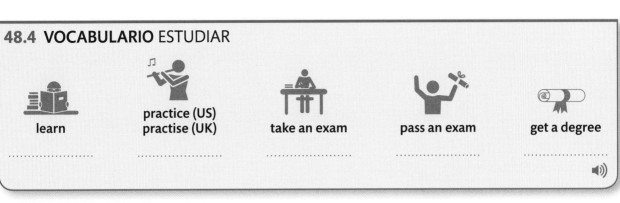

48.4 VOCABULARIO ESTUDIAR

learn	practice (US) practise (UK)	take an exam	pass an exam	get a degree

....

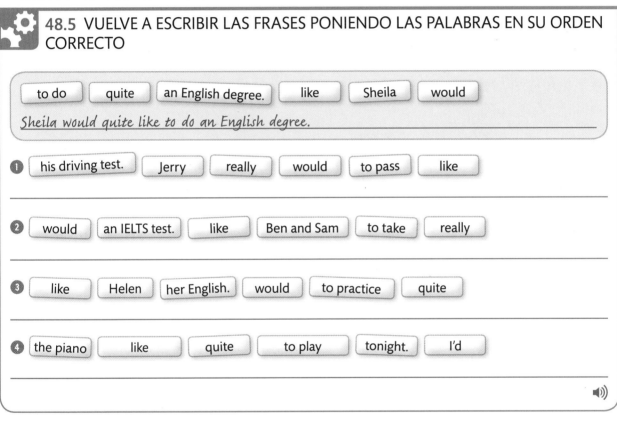

48.5 VUELVE A ESCRIBIR LAS FRASES PONIENDO LAS PALABRAS EN SU ORDEN CORRECTO

to do | quite | an English degree. | like | Sheila | would

Sheila would quite like to do an English degree.

① his driving test. | Jerry | really | would | to pass | like

_____

② would | an IELTS test. | like | Ben and Sam | to take | really

_____

③ like | Helen | her English. | would | to practice | quite

_____

④ the piano | like | quite | to play | tonight. | I'd

_____

48.6 UTILIZA EL DIAGRAMA PARA CREAR 12 FRASES CORRECTAS Y DILAS EN VOZ ALTA

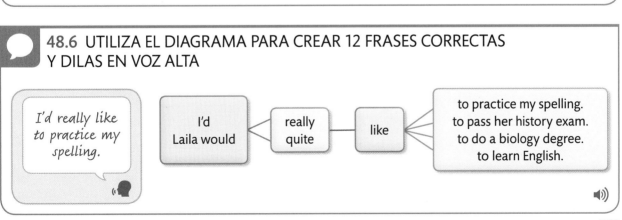

I'd really like to practice my spelling.

| I'd
Laila would | really
quite | like | to practice my spelling.
to pass her history exam.
to do a biology degree.
to learn English. |

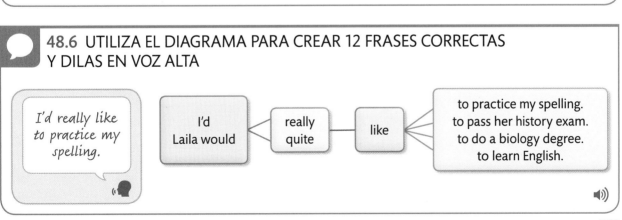

48.7 PUNTO CLAVE LA OMISIÓN DEL ARTÍCULO

Cuando hables sobre el uso de algunos lugares e instituciones, no es necesario utilizar un artículo ("a" o "the").

Ella va allí para estudiar, que es la finalidad de una escuela, así que no hace falta poner el artículo.

Liz is seven. She goes to school now.

Larry works at the school in Park Street.

Utiliza el artículo para referirte al edificio específico en el que trabaja.

48.8 MÁS EJEMPLOS LA OMISIÓN DEL ARTÍCULO

SIN ARTÍCULO

I am at university in Chicago.

Pierre is in hospital.

Liz goes to church on Sundays.

Go to bed, Tom!

Sue is in town this afternoon.

Sarah studies at home.

ARTÍCULO

The University of Chicago is good.

The hospital is far away.

St. Mary's is an old church.

Your shirt is on the bed.

Hancock is a nice town.

This dog hasn't got a home.

48.9 TACHA LAS PALABRAS INCORRECTAS DE CADA FRASE

Sheila works at ~~school~~ / the school near here.

① Emily has **lovely home** / a lovely home.

② Sue always takes her lunch to **office** / the office.

③ Can you see where **church** / the church is?

④ Jim went to **bed** / the bed hours ago.

⑤ Can you drive me into **town** / a town later?

⑥ I live next to **university** / the university.

⑦ I leave **home** / a home at 8am every weekday.

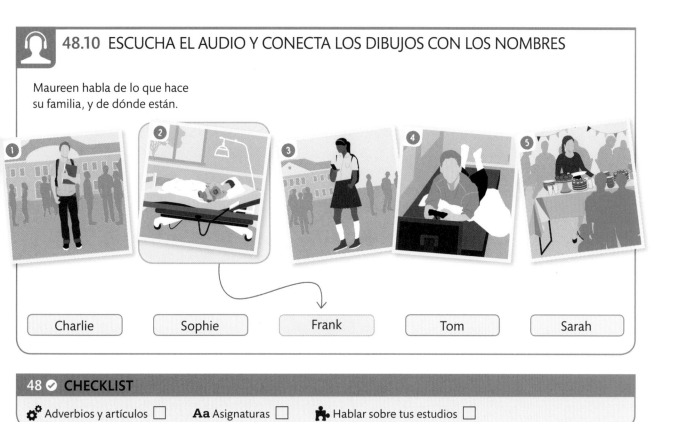

48.10 ESCUCHA EL AUDIO Y CONECTA LOS DIBUJOS CON LOS NOMBRES

Maureen habla de lo que hace
su familia, y de dónde están.

Charlie | Sophie | Frank | Tom | Sarah

---

48 ✓ CHECKLIST

⚙ Adverbios y artículos ☐   **Aa** Asignaturas ☐   🧩 Hablar sobre tus estudios ☐

♻ REPASA LO QUE HAS APRENDIDO EN LAS UNIDADES 43–48

NUEVO LENGUAJE	FRASES DE EJEMPLO	☑	UNIDAD
"CAN", "CANNOT" Y "CAN'T"	I can **ride a bicycle**. He can **play guitar**. I cannot / can't **sing jazz songs**.	☐	44.1, 44.3, 44.7
UTILIZAR ADVERBIOS	I **speak** quietly. He **speaks** loudly.	☐	45.1, 45.4
"GOOD AT" Y "BAD AT"	**She's** good at **running**. **I am** bad at **making cakes**.	☐	45.7, 45.8
ADVERBIOS MODIFICADORES	I **can ski** quite **well**. She **can ski** very **well**. She **can ski** really **well**.	☐	46.1, 46.4
"I WOULD LIKE" Y "I WANT"	He wants **to write a book**. I would like **to climb a mountain**.	☐	47.1, 47.7
"REALLY" Y "QUITE"	I love music. I'd really **like to study it this term**. I like biology. I'd quite **like to study it next year**.	☐	48.2, 48.3
LA OMISIÓN DEL ARTÍCULO	**My daughter goes** to school **now**.	☐	48.7, 48.8

Respuestas

1.4 🔊
1. I'm Charlotte.
2. My name's Una.
3. My name's Simone.
4. I'm Carlos.
5. I'm Juan.
6. My name's Miriam.
7. I'm Sarah.

1.5
Ⓐ 5
Ⓑ 1
Ⓒ 2
Ⓓ 3
Ⓔ 6
Ⓕ 4

1.6 🔊
1. Hi! My name is Linda.
2. Hi! My name is Abdul.
3. Hi! My name is Paolo.
4. Hello! My name is Linda.
5. Hello! My name is Abdul.
6. Hello! My name is Paolo.
7. Hi! I am Linda.
8. Hi! I am Abdul.
9. Hi! I am Paolo.
10. Hello! I am Linda.
11. Hello! I am Abdul.
12. Hello! I am Paolo.

1.9
1. B-E-L-I-N-D-A
2. L-E-W-I-S
3. A-D-A-M-S
4. B-O-B
5. S-P-E-N-C-E-R
6. K-A-T-E W-A-L-L-A-C-E
7. S-A-U-L J-A-C-K-S-O-N
8. N-A-T-A-L-I-E L-A-U
9. C-H-R-I-S B-O-Y-L-E

1.10 🔊
1. B-A-S-H-I-R
2. B-E-N J-A-M-E-S
3. M-O-L-L-Y
4. L-O-P-E-Z
5. N-A-D-I-Y-A L-A-T-I-F

3.5 🔊
1. eleven
2. seventeen
3. thirty-four
4. fifty-nine
5. eighty-five

3.6 🔊
1. Theo **is** 45 years old.
2. Madison **is** 27 years old.
3. Jeremy and Tanya **are** 90 years old.
4. We **are** 29 years old.
5. I **am** 34 years old.

3.8
1. 40
2. 30
3. 19
4. 60
5. 80
6. 17
7. 13

3.12
1. Japan
2. US
3. France

3.13 🔊
1. Spanish
2. German
3. Canadian
4. American
5. Australian
6. Chinese

3.14 🔊
1. I am Australian.
2. I am English.
3. I am from Italy.
4. I am from France.
5. You are Australian.
6. You are English.
7. You are from Italy.
8. You are from France.
9. They are Australian.
10. They are English.
11. They are from Italy.
12. They are from France.

5.3 🔊
1. your horse
2. their sheep
3. our fish

4. its bone
5. his dog

5.4 🔊
1. Bingo is **my** dog.
2. **Her** aunt is called Goldie.
3. **My** cat eats fish.
4. **Their** rabbit lives in the backyard.
5. **Our** parrot is from Colombia.
6. **His** wife is called Henrietta.
7. **Their** dog is 10 years old.
8. **Our** aunt lives on a farm in Ohio.
9. Here is **its** ball.

5.5 🔊
1. Farida **is** their sister.
2. Duke **is** our dog.
3. Daisy **is** her mother.
4. They **are** his grandparents.
5. It **is** our horse.
6. John **is** our cousin.
7. I **am** Daisy's daughter.
8. You **are** my friend.

5.8 🔊
1. **This** is her horse.
2. **That** is our rabbit.
3. **That** is their pig.
4. **This** is his cow.
5. **This** is your fish.

5.9 🔊
1. Lily is their sister.
2. Our son is 12 years old.
3. That is their cow.
4. This is your ball.
5. Her father is called Caspar.

5.10
Ⓐ 2
Ⓑ 1
Ⓒ 5
Ⓓ 3
Ⓔ 4

5.11 🔊
1. This is my cat.
2. This is my parrot.
3. This is her cat.
4. This is her parrot.
5. This is their cat.
6. This is their parrot.
7. That is my cat.
8. That is my parrot.
9. That is her cat.
10. That is her parrot.
11. That is their cat.
12. That is their parrot.

06

6.3 🔊
1 Ben's son
2 Sam and Ayshah's cat
3 Debbie's house
4 Marco and Kate's car
5 Elsa's grandchild
6 Beth's parrot

6.4
1 Lucas is Ben's father.
2 Lily is Ben's mother.
3 Noah is Ben's son.
4 Grace is Ben's sister.
5 Alex is Ben's brother.

6.7 🔊
1 Angela is Skanda's wife.
2 That is my cousins' snake.
3 Sue is Ella and Mark's aunt.
4 Ginger is John's cat.

6.8 🔊
1 Kathy is **Dave's** aunt.
2 Rex is **Noah and Pat's** dog.
3 This is **her cousins'** house.
4 Felix is **the children's** cat.

08

8.2 🔊
1 **These** are Diego's keys.
2 **This** is Olivia's purse.
3 **Those** are my books.
4 **These** are my pencils.
5 **That** is Anna's sandwich.
6 **That** is Malik's phone.

8.3
1 That is his apple.
2 Those are her pens.
3 That is my ring.
4 These are our keys.
5 That is his brother.
6 These are my pencils.

8.5 🔊
PLURALES EN "s":
1. apples, 2. bottles, 3. necklaces
PLURALES EN "es":
4. sandwiches, 5. brushes, 6. watches
PLURALES EN "ies":
7. dictionaries, 8. diaries

8.6 🔊
1 watches
2 books
3 sandwiches
4 toothbrushes
5 necklaces
6 apples
7 keys
8 cell phones

8.9
1 This is her laptop. This laptop is hers.
2 Those are their keys. Those keys are theirs.
3 These are our passports. These passports are ours.
4 That is his brush. That brush is his.

8.10
CARTERA DE TOM:
sandwiches, cell phone, ID card, chocolate bar.
CARTERA DE SARAH:
purse, books, brush, notebook.

8.11 🔊
1. Those are my books.
2. Those are my dogs.
3. That is my brother.
4. These are my books.
5. These are my dogs.
6. This is my brother.
7. Those are Bruno's books.
8. Those are Bruno's dogs.
9. That is Bruno's brother.
10. These are Bruno's books.
11. These are Bruno's dogs.
12. This is Bruno's brother.

10

10.2 🔊
1 You **are a** doctor.
2 She **is a** farmer.
3 They **are** teachers.
4 We **are** nurses.
5 I **am an** actor.
6 She **is a** chef.

10.3 🔊
1 You **are** a driver.
2 I **am** a mechanic.
3 He **is** a vet.
4 We **are** sales assistants.
5 They **are** businesswomen.
6 She **is** a waitress.
7 We **are** receptionists.
8 She **is** a gardener.

10.5 🔊
1 hospital
2 farm
3 laboratory
4 restaurant
5 school
6 construction site
7 hospital
8 theater
9 restaurant

10.7
1 False 2 False 3 True 4 True

10.9
A 3
B 4
C 1
D 6
E 5
F 2

10.10 🔊
1 She **is a builder. She works on a construction site.**
2 We **are scientists. We work in a laboratory.**
3 You **are an actor. You work in a theater.**
4 He **is a waiter. He works in a restaurant.**
5 Chloe **is a nurse. She works in a hospital.**

10.13
1 Noah's mother
2 Noah's sister
3 Noah's father
4 Noah's brother

10.14 🔊
1 Selma **is a chef. She works with** food.
2 Max **is a** nurse. **He works with** patients.
3 Mat **is a** mechanic. **He works with** cars.
4 Ana **is a** vet. **She works with** animals.
5 Jazmin **is a** judge. **She works with** people.

11

11.3 🔊
1 It's midnight.
2 It's half past three.
3 It's quarter to twelve.
4 It's two thirty.
5 It's a quarter past nine.
6 It's ten thirty.

11.4
1 11:30
2 7:00
3 4:15
4 9:30
5 2:15

11.5 🔊
1. 9:00
2. 1:15
3. 3:25
4. 2:30
5. 12:15

11.6 🔊
1. It's half past five. / It's five thirty.
2. It's a quarter to seven. / It's six forty-five.
3. It's twenty-five to twelve. / It's eleven thirty-five.
4. It's a quarter past eight. / It's eight fifteen.
5. It's twenty-two past ten. / It's ten twenty-two.

13

13.4 🔊
1. He **wakes** up at 7 o'clock.
2. You **leave** home at 8:30am.
3. I **start** work at 10am.
4. Ellen **gets** up at 5 o'clock.
5. My wife **takes** a shower in the evening.
6. I **take** a shower in the morning.
7. My parents **eat** lunch at 2pm.
8. We **leave** work at 4pm.
9. My brother **works** with animals.

13.5 🔊
1. I **leave** work at 5:30pm.
2. Phil **eats** lunch at 12:30pm.
3. We **get** up at 8am.
4. His son **starts** work at 5am.
5. My sister **leaves** work at 7pm.
6. They **eat** dinner at 10pm.

13.6 🔊
1. My son **wakes** up at 5am.
2. I **leave** work at 6:30pm.
3. We **eat** breakfast at 8am.
4. Paula **works** outside.
5. My wife **starts** work at 7am.
6. He **eats** lunch at noon.

13.9 🔊
1. washes
2. watches
3. wakes
4. goes
5. finishes
6. leaves

13.10 🔊
1. Lucia **wakes** up at 7am.
2. I **get** up at 7:30am.
3. Ethan **goes** to work at 5am.
4. You **leave** work at 5pm.
5. Shona **watches** TV in the evening.

13.11 🔊
1. My mother **watches** TV in the morning.
2. We **go** to bed at midnight.
3. My husband **finishes** work at 6:30pm.
4. Rob **goes** to work at 8:30am.
5. I **take** a shower in the morning.
6. I **leave** work at 6 o'clock in the evening.

13.12
1. True
2. True
3. False
4. False
5. True
6. True

13.13 🔊
1. I start work at noon.
2. I finish work at noon.
3. My brother starts work at noon.
4. My brother finishes work at noon.
5. They start work at noon.
6. They finish work at noon.
7. I start work at 2:30pm.
8. I finish work at 2:30pm.
9. My brother starts work at 2:30pm.
10. My brother finishes work at 2:30pm.
11. They start work at 2:30pm.
12. They finish work at 2:30pm.

14

14.3 🔊
1. We eat lunch at 3pm **on** the weekend / **at** the weekend.
2. She goes to bed at 1am **on** the weekend / **at** the weekend.
3. I go to work **from** Monday **to** Wednesday.
4. They eat dinner at 9pm **on** the weekend / **at** the weekend.
5. We finish work at 3pm **on** Fridays.
6. I eat breakfast at work **on** Mondays.

14.5 🔊
1. He **goes to the gym** on Tuesdays and Fridays.
2. They **go swimming** on Thursdays.
3. He **plays soccer** on Wednesdays.
4. I **take a bath** on the weekend.
5. You **read the newspaper** on Saturdays.

14.6 🔊
1. I watch TV **on** Sundays.
2. I take a bath **at** 7pm every day.
3. I go to bed **at** 10 o'clock **on** Sundays.
4. I get up **at** 8am **from** Monday to Friday.

14.10
1. True 2. True 3. False 4. True
5. False

14.11 🔊
1. I get up at 6am five days a week.
2. They go to bed at 11pm every day.
3. Sarah plays soccer twice a week.
4. Jamie washes his clothes once a week.

14.12 🔊
1. We get up **at** 7am five times a week.
2. They go to work **from** Monday to Friday.
3. Linda washes her face **every** day.
4. Colin sleeps **from** 11pm **to** 6am.

15

15.4 🔊
1. She is not my sister.
2. That is not her car.
3. I am not 35 years old.
4. We are not Spanish.
5. Chad is not a vet.

15.5 🔊
1. He **is not** in the office.
2. She **is not** a businesswoman.
3. I **am not** 18 years old.
4. This **is not** a snake.
5. We **are not** artists.
6. You **are not** at work.
7. Dexter **is not** a cat.

15.6
A. 3
B. 1
C. 5
D. 2
E. 4

15.9 🔊
1. It **is not** 10 o'clock in the morning.
2. You **aren't** 35 years old.
3. I **am not** Australian.
4. My brother **isn't** married.
5. Tom and Angela **aren't** construction workers.

15.10
1. True
2. True
3. False
4. True
5. False
6. True
7. False

15.11 🔊
1. I am not at work.
2. I am not tired.
3. I am not 24 years old.
4. You aren't at work.
5. You aren't tired.
6. You aren't 24 years old.

7. He isn't at work.
8. He isn't tired.
9. He isn't 24 years old.
10. They aren't at work.
11. They aren't tired.
12. They aren't 24 years old.

16

16.4 🔊
1 I **do not** read the papers on Saturday.
2 The dog **does not** eat fish.
3 They **do not** go to the theater often.
4 Ben and I **do not** live on a farm now.
5 Theo **does not** cycle to work.
6 You **do not** work at Fabio's café.
7 Claire **does not** watch TV in the evening.
8 We **do not** play football at home.
9 Pierre **does not** wake up before noon.

16.5
1 False
2 True
3 False
4 False

16.8
1 We go to work every day. We do not go to work every day.
2 He watches TV in the evening. He doesn't watch TV in the evening.
3 You do not work in an office. You don't work in an office.
4 They play tennis. They do not play tennis.
5 She works with children. She doesn't work with children.

16.9 🔊
1 We don't work with animals.
2 I don't eat chocolate.
3 Sandy doesn't work in a hairdresser's.
4 Melanie and Cris don't have a car.
5 They don't live in Park Road now.
6 We don't watch Hollywood movies.
7 She doesn't drive a taxi.

16.10 🔊
1. I don't work outside.
2. I don't have a bicycle.
3. I don't play tennis.
4. You don't work outside.
5. You don't have a bicycle.
6. You don't play tennis.
7. We don't work outside.
8. We don't have a bicycle.
9. We don't play tennis.
10. Meg doesn't work outside.
11. Meg doesn't have a bicycle.
12. Meg doesn't play tennis.

16.11
1 Kim
2 Selma
3 Chiyo
4 Maria
5 Selma

17

17.4 🔊
1 Is Brad a nurse?
2 Are these my keys?
3 Are Ruby and Farid actors?
4 Is this his laptop?
5 Is Valeria his sister?

17.5
1 A
2 B
3 B
4 A
5 A
6 B

17.7 🔊
1 **Is** Holly your mother?
2 **Are** they from Argentina?
3 **Are** you a teacher?
4 **Is** this your dog?
5 **Is** there a post office?

17.11 🔊
1 **Do** you get up at 7am?
2 **Do** they live at number 59?
3 **Do** we finish work at 6pm today?
4 **Does** the parrot talk all day?
5 **Do** you work in a lab?

17.12 🔊
1 Do you live in New York?
2 Does she work on a farm?
3 Does he get up at 5am every day?
4 Do they come from Peru?
5 Does Brad work in the post office?

17.13 🔊
1 Do they live in New York City?
2 Does he work in a restaurant?
3 Does Lewis go swimming on Fridays?
4 Does Marisha work with animals?

17.14 🔊
1 **Does** she go swimming on Tuesdays?
2 **Do** you read the paper on Sundays?
3 **Does** she work with animals?
4 **Do** they work on a construction site?

18

18.3
1 True
2 False
3 False
4 True
5 False

18.4 🔊
1 No, it isn't.
2 Yes, it is.
3 Yes, she does.
4 No, I don't.
5 No, it isn't.

18.5 🔊
1 No, **I'm not**
2 Yes, **they do.**
3 No, **it isn't.**
4 Yes, **she does.**
5 No, **she isn't.**
6 Yes, **they do.**
7 No, **he isn't.**

19

19.3 🔊
1 What **are** their names?
2 What **is** the time?
3 What **are** my favorite colors?
4 What **is** the hotel next to?
5 What **are** they?
6 What **is** your uncle's name?
7 What **is** my name?

19.6 🔊
1 What is the time? It's 5 o'clock.
2 When is your birthday? July 23.
3 Which is your car? The red Ferrari.
4 Why are you here? For a meeting.
5 How old are you? I'm 25.
6 Who is there? It's me, Marcus.

19.7 🔊
1 **Where** are your parents from?
2 **How** old are you?
3 **When** is breakfast?
4 **Who** is your friend talking to?
5 **Why** is it cold in here?
6 **Which** person is your teacher?

19.11 🔊
1 When **does** she eat lunch?
2 Where **do** they live?
3 Which bag **do** you want?
4 Where **does** he come from?
5 When **does** the movie end?

19.12 🔊
1 Where does he play football?
2 When do you clean the car?
3 What time does the party start?
4 Which days do you play tennis?

19.13
1 When do you eat breakfast?
2 What do you study?
3 Where do you work?
4 Who is she?

19.14 🔊
1 **Where** do you work in the city?
2 **When** do you start work?
3 **What** time does it open?
4 **How** many people do you work with?
5 **Who** do you work with?

19.15
1 Her brother
2 Two
3 At 7am
4 Goes swimming
5 By the pool
6 Tomorrow

19.16 🔊
1. Where does Kate play golf?
2. Where do they play golf
3. Where do you play golf?
4. Where does Kate go to the gym?
5. Where do they go to the gym?
6. Where do you go to the gym?
7. When does Kate play golf?
8. When do they play golf?
9. When do you play golf?
10. When does Kate go to the gym?
11. When do they go to the gym?
12. When do you go to the gym?

19.17 🔊
1 How often **do** they play tennis?
2 Which office **does** he work in?
3 Where **is** the party?
4 What **do** you do?

19.18 🔊
1 What **is her cat called**?
2 Who **is your English teacher**?
3 Where **does Ben work**?
4 How **is your grandmother**?

21

21.3 🔊
1 **There are** two churches.
2 **There is** a swimming pool.
3 **There is** a library.
4 **There are** two castles.

21.4
1 airports
2 theaters
3 schools
4 hospitals
5 bars
6 churches
7 factories
8 offices

21.5 🔊
1 There are two schools.
2 There are two cafés.
3 There is a hospital.
4 There is a restaurant.
5 There are three stores.

21.7 🔊
1 There **isn't** a theater.
2 There **aren't** any factories.
3 There **isn't** a bus station.
4 There **aren't** any airports.
5 There **aren't** any churches.

21.10 🔊
1 There **are** no castles.
2 There **aren't** any factories.
3 There **are** no hospitals.
4 There **aren't** any churches.
5 There **are** no swimming pools.
6 There **are** no airports.

21.11
A 3
B 1
C 2
D 4

21.12
1 True
2 False
3 False
4 True

21.13 🔊
1 **There isn't** a park.
2 **There is** a hotel.
3 **There are** no cafés.
4 **There isn't** an airport.
5 **There are** two stores.
6 **There isn't** a train station.
7 **There are** two theaters.

22

22.3 🔊
1 **The** new teacher is called Miss Jones.
2 There is **a** good café in the park.
3 I work at **the** hotel next to the library.
4 There is **a** swimming pool near my office.
5 It is **the** dog's favorite toy.

6 Janie is **an** artist at the gallery.
7 See you at **the** café at the bus station.

22.6 🔊
1 There are **some** stores on Broad Street.
2 There is **a** café next to the castle.
3 There are **some** cakes on the table.
4 There is **a** phone here.
5 There are **some** factories downtown.

22.7 🔊
1 There **are** some supermarkets in town.
2 There **is** an office near the river.
3 There **are** some chocolate bars in my bag.
4 There **is** a hospital near the bus station.

22.10 🔊
1 Are there **any** stores on your street?
2 Is there **an** airport near Littleton?
3 Are there **any** mosques in the city?
4 Is there **a** swimming pool downtown?
5 Are there **any** offices in that building?

22.11 🔊
1 Is there a supermarket near here?
2 Are there any cafés on Elm Road?
3 Are there any hotels near your house?
4 Is there a café near your office?
5 Is there a bar next to the bank?

22.13 🔊
1 Yes, **there is.**
2 Yes, **there are.**
3 No, **there isn't.**
4 Yes, **there are.**
5 No, **there isn't.**
6 No, **there aren't.**

22.14 🔊
1 Yes, there are.
2 No, there isn't.
3 No, there aren't.
4 Yes, there is.

23

23.3 🔊
1 Wake up
2 Do
3 Start
4 Have
5 Wait
6 Stop
7 Work

23.5 🔊
1 Take the second right. The station is on the left.
2 Take the first left, then turn right. The restaurant is on the right.
3 Take the second left, and the hospital is on the right.

④ Take the first left, then go straight ahead. The hotel is on the right.
⑤ Take the first left, then turn left. The castle is on the right.

23.7 🔊
① The supermarket is **next to** the post office.
② The museum is **behind** the café.
③ The station is **in front of** the church.
④ The cinema is on the **corner** of the intersection.
⑤ The post office is **between** the café and the supermarket.

23.10 🔊
① Don't read that book.
② Don't go past the hotel.
③ Don't give that to the cat.
④ Don't have a shower.
⑤ Don't drive to the mall.

23.11
① Library
② Swimming pool
③ Movie theater
④ Science museum

24

24.3 🔊
① There are two hotels and three shops.
② Hilda works in a school and a theater.
③ My uncle is a scientist and my aunt is a doctor.
④ Sue watches TV and she reads books.
⑤ The store opens at night and Jan starts work.

24.4
Ⓐ 3
Ⓒ 1
Ⓓ 4
Ⓔ 2

24.6 🔊
① There are hotels, bars, and stores.
② Sam eats breakfast, lunch, and dinner.
③ I play tennis, soccer, and chess.
④ Teo plays with his car, train, and bus.
⑤ There is a pencil, a bag, and a cell phone.
⑥ My friends, girlfriend, and aunt are here.
⑦ Ling works on Monday, Thursday, and Friday.

24.8 🔊
① This is my car, but these aren't my car keys.
② We eat a small breakfast, but we eat a big lunch.
③ I work from Monday to Friday, but not on the weekend.
④ The bathroom has a shower, but it doesn't have a bathtub.

24.9 🔊
① There isn't a bathtub, but there is a shower.
② There isn't a bar, but there is a café.
③ The bag is Maya's, but that laptop isn't hers.
④ Si doesn't have any dogs, but he has two cats.
⑤ Sally reads books, but she never watches TV.

24.10 🔊
① Lu reads books **and** magazines.
② I work every weekday, **but** not on weekends.
③ Jim is a husband **and** a father.
④ There is a cinema, **but** no theater.
⑤ There isn't a gym, **but** there is a pool.

24.11 🔊
① There is a cat and a rabbit, but there isn't a snake.
② There is a doctor and a builder, but not a chef.
③ There is a laptop and a newspaper, but there isn't a cell phone.
④ There is a movie theater and a restaurant, but not a theater.

25

25.3 🔊
① He is a horrible man.
② They are small children.
③ My uncle is a quiet man.
④ There is a large cake.
⑤ These are my old shoes.
⑥ There is a new supermarket.
⑦ You work in an old museum.

25.5
1. **small** 2. **beautiful** 3. **old** 4. **large** 5. **busy**
6. **horrible** 7. **beautiful**

25.6
① The nurse is busy. She is busy.
② The dog is quiet. He is quiet.
③ The patients are new. They are new.
④ The town is horrible. It is horrible.
⑤ The car is beautiful. It is beautiful.

25.8
① beautiful
② lake
③ large
④ mountains
⑤ restaurant
⑥ beach
⑦ busy
⑧ quiet

25.9 🔊
① **The** countryside **is** quiet **and the** trees **are** beautiful.
② **The** city **is** horrible **and the** people **are** busy.
③ **The** hotel **is** new **and the** swimming pool **is** large.

④ **The** beach **is** big **and the** cafés **are** busy.
⑤ **The** city **is** old **and the** buildings **are** beautiful.

25.12
Ⓐ 2
Ⓑ 5
Ⓒ 1
Ⓓ 4
Ⓔ 3
Ⓕ 6

25.13 🔊
① There are **lots of** people.
② There are **some** buildings.
③ There are **a few** cars.
④ There are **a few** parks.

25.14 🔊
① In the tree, there are a few birds and some apples.
② In the sea, there are a few people and lots of fish.
③ In the countryside, there are some people and lots of trees.

26

26.3
① lives there.
② she's a farmer.
③ goes swimming.
④ it's new.
⑤ with people.
⑥ her aunt lives there.
⑦ lots of people.

26.4 🔊
① She lives on a farm because **she's a farmer**.
② She works in a hotel because **she's a receptionist**.
③ They get up late because **they're students**.
④ We work with children because **we're teachers**.
⑤ You don't eat lunch because **you're busy**.
⑥ I work outside because **I'm a gardener**.
⑦ My parents go to the country because **it's quiet**.

28

28.3 🔊
① They **have** a car.
② You **have** a chair.
③ He **has** a dog.
④ We **have** a daughter.
⑤ It **has** a door.

28.4
① Maya ② Ben ③ Ben ④ Ben

28.5
1 False
2 True
3 False
4 False
5 True
6 True

28.7 🔊
1 Kaleh does not have a dog.
2 You don't have a microwave.
3 Greendale does not have a church.
4 Alyssa and Logan don't have a garage.
5 We do not have a yard.

28.8 🔊
1. I have a couch.
2. I have some chairs.
3. I have a dining room.
4. We have a couch.
5. We have some chairs.
6. We have a dining room.
7. She has a couch.
8. She has some chairs.
9. She has a dining room.
10. She doesn't have a couch.
11. She doesn't have a dining room.

28.11
1 They have not got a couch. They haven't got a couch.
2 He has got three sisters. He's got three sisters.
3 You have not got a bike. You haven't got a bike.
4 We have got a microwave. We've got a microwave.
5 It has got a bathtub. It's got a bathtub.
6 They have got a cat. They've got a cat.

29

29.3 🔊
1 Do they have a toaster?
2 Do you have a new couch?
3 Does Ben have a washing machine?
4 Do we have an old armchair?
5 Does Karen have a large TV?
6 Does the kitchen have a sink?
7 Does the house have a yard?

29.4
1 Lucy
2 Lucy
3 Lucy
4 Tim
5 Tim

29.5 🔊
1. Do you have any chairs?
2. Do you have a kettle?
3. Do you have any plates?
4. Do they have any chairs?
5. Do they have a kettle?
6. Do they have any plates?
7. Does he have any chairs?
8. Does he have a kettle?
9. Does he have any plates?

29.7 🔊
1 No, I don't.
2 Yes, I do.
3 Yes, I do.
4 No, I don't.

29.8 🔊
1 No, he doesn't.
2 No, he doesn't.
3 Yes, he does.

29.10 🔊
1 Has this town got a theater?
2 Has your house got an attic?
3 Have they got laptops?
4 Has this coffee shop got a bathroom?
5 Have you got a cell phone?
6 Has the teacher got my book?

29.11 🔊
1 Yes, **she has**.
2 Yes, **it has**.
3 No, **they haven't**.
4 No, **it hasn't**.

31

31.3 🔊
1 Jake has **an** apple.
2 There is **some** coffee.
3 Reena eats **some** spaghetti.
4 There are **some** eggs.
5 I've got **some** bananas.

31.5
1 There is some milk. There isn't any milk.
2 Is there any chocolate? There isn't any chocolate.
3 Are there any apples? There are some apples.

31.6 🔊
1 Yes, **there is**.
2 No, **there aren't**.
3 No, **there isn't**.

31.9 🔊
1 There is **a bag of** flour.
2 There is **a cup of** coffee.
3 There is **a carton of** juice.
4 There are **two bowls of** spaghetti.
5 There are **two glasses of** milk.

31.12 🔊
1 **How many** glasses of juice are there?
2 **How much** water is there?
3 **How many** potatoes are there?
4 **How many** bars of chocolate are there?
5 **How much** pasta is there?
6 **How many** cartons of juice are there?
7 **How much** milk is there?

31.13
1 one bag
2 three
3 some
4 cheese

32

32.3 🔊
1 There **are enough** oranges.
2 You have **enough** pineapples.
3 There **are too many** apples.
4 You don't have **enough** bananas.

32.6
1 Too many
2 Not enough
3 Enough
4 Too much

32.7 🔊
1 There is **too much** sugar.
2 They **don't have** enough butter.
3 She has **too many** mangoes.
4 John has too many **eggs**.
5 There **aren't** enough oranges.
6 That is **too much** flour.
7 There **is** too much sugar in the cake.

34

34.2 🔊
1 Hannah **chooses** a yellow skirt.
2 Elliot and Ruby **buy** a new couch.
3 Sue **owns** an old winter coat.
4 Jess's dad **buys** her a new bike.
5 Chris and Lisa **own** a black sports car.
6 Gayle and Mike **sell** shoes at the market.
7 Mia **chooses** her red shoes.
8 The shoes **fit** me.
9 We **want** new white shirts.

34.3 🔊
1 They choose expensive blue sweaters.
2 Judith has some old brown hats.
3 This shop sells short red pants.
4 Tina owns cheap black shoes.
5 Jim buys a new black coat.

34.4

1. **new** 2. **cheap** 3. **white** 4. **long** 5. **black**
6. **black** 7. **old** 8. **new** 9. **expensive** 10. **cheap**
11. **red** 12. **long**

34.5

1. a blue hat
2. a new t-shirt
3. a cheap skirt
4. a black coat

34.7

1. too cheap
2. too expensive
3. too long
4. too short
5. too old
6. too new
7. too big

34.8 ◀))

1. Jim's pants are **too short**.
2. Sam's dress is **too long**.
3. Molly's sweater is **too small**.
4. Helen's red hat is **too big**.
5. Lili's shoes are **too big**.

34.9

1. B
2. A
3. B
4. A
5. A

34.10 ◀))

1. These black pants are too big.
2. These black pants are big enough.
3. These black pants are too short.
4. My expensive pants are too big.
5. My expensive pants are big enough.
6. My expensive pants are too short.
7. My black dress is too big.
8. My black dress is big enough.
9. My black dress is too short.
10. My expensive dress is too big.
11. My expensive dress is big enough.
12. My expensive dress is too short.

35

35.4 ◀))

1. This is a **horrible** old t-shirt.
2. This is a **boring** movie.
3. I have a **lovely** long dress.
4. This is a **beautiful** bird.
5. This is a **fun** party.

35.5 ◀))

1. That is a horrible blue car.
2. This is a fun short story.
3. I have a lovely black cat.

---

4. He has an ugly red house.
5. They own a great new laptop.

35.6

1. A
2. B
3. A
4. A

35.8 ◀))

1. Oh, no, the blue glass vase!
2. We have two plastic chairs.
3. What an interesting metal box!
4. That's an expensive leather couch.

35.9 ◀))

1. She owns some beautiful wooden chairs.
2. We don't own those horrible plastic plates.
3. They have an ugly yellow car.
4. He wears a boring blue sweater.
5. She wants a new metal lamp.
6. He owns a large fabric bag.
7. Norah wants a new leather jacket.

37

37.3 ◀))

1. We don't **go surfing** in the winter.
2. Do you **go sailing** on the weekend?
3. Tipo **goes cycling** five times a week.
4. He **goes fishing** on the river.
5. Sharon **goes dancing** with her friend.
6. Do they **go running** every morning?
7. He doesn't **go horse riding**.

37.4

1. Wednesday
2. Friday
3. Tuesday
4. Thursday

37.6 ◀))

GERUNDIOS REGULARES:
sailing, snowboarding, skateboarding
GERUNDIOS CON DOBLE CONSONANTE:
swimming, running, shopping
GERUNDIOS QUE HAN PERDIDO LA LETRA "E":
skating, horse riding, cycling

37.9 ◀))

1. Shala **doesn't play** tennis.
2. Mina **plays** golf at the club.
3. We **play** squash on Mondays.
4. The dog **plays** with its ball.
5. Maria **doesn't play** tennis.
6. The kids **don't play** games at school.
7. They **play** soccer at the park.

37.10 ◀))

1. We **play** tennis every Tuesday night.
2. They **don't play** golf during the week.
3. You **don't play** volleyball at the beach.
4. Do they **play** together every Saturday?

37.11

1. Sara
2. Chas
3. Sara
4. Cassie

37.12 ◀))

1. Milo and I **go cycling** in the park on Saturdays.
2. The team **plays /play football** from 6pm to 7pm on Wednesdays.
3. Imelda **goes horse riding** once a month.
4. Luther **goes fishing** during his vacation time.
5. Hannah **plays tennis** with her cousin on Monday evenings.

39

39.3 ◀))

1. We never go to the mall.
2. Sally and Ken usually cycle to work.
3. My sister often works outside.

39.4

1. usually
2. never
3. usually
4. often
5. always

39.5 ◀))

1. Nico **usually** swims after work. He **never** watches TV on the weekend.
2. Meg **often** goes surfing in Hawaii. She **sometimes** dances all night.
3. Alma **always** reads on vacation. She **sometimes** plays golf on Sundays.
4. Carrie **usually** goes to bed late and she **never** eats breakfast.

39.8 ◀))

1. How often do they go to work?
2. When do you get up?
3. How often do you go on vacation?
4. When do they go shopping?
5. How often do you visit Mischa?

39.9 ◀))

1. When do they visit their grandparents?
2. When do we go skating?
3. How often does he play hockey?
4. When do you go shopping?
5. How often do they see their parents?
6. How often does he walk the dog?
7. How often do we go skating on the lake?

39.10 🔊
1. When do you do yoga?
2. How often do you go to the movies?
3. How often do you go skateboarding?
4. When do you arrive at work?
5. How often do you go surfing?

40

40.3 🔊
1. Ava and Elsa love the mountains.
2. Shania hates mice.
3. Manuel likes his book.
4. Cats don't like the rain.

40.4
1. Imelda doesn't hate pasta.
2. My dog doesn't love steak.
3. Our grandfather doesn't like coffee.
4. I don't love the sea.
5. Sam and Jen don't hate hockey.
6. You don't like the countryside.
7. We don't like our new cell phones.

40.5
1. hockey
2. some actors
3. pizza
4. spiders

40.6 🔊
1. I love cats.
2. I love curry.
3. I love this house.
4. You love cats.
5. You love curry.
6. You love this house.
7. Milly hates cats.
8. Milly hates curry.
9. Milly hates this house.

40.9
1. D
2. B
3. C
4. A

40.10
1. True
2. False
3. False
4. True
5. False
6. True
7. False
8. True
9. True

40.14 🔊
1. Why does Una love skiing?
2. Why do they like this book?
3. Why doesn't Debbie like her job?
4. Do we like cooking?
5. Does she love surfing?
6. Do I hate working late?
7. Does Aziz love Ontario?

40.15 🔊
1. I like English class because it's interesting.
2. We love skating because it's exciting.
3. He hates cleaning because it's boring.

42

42.3
1. basketball
2. fish
3. Rome
4. gardener
5. Italian
6. running
7. cooking

42.4
1. A
2. B
3. A
4. C
5. A

42.5 🔊
1. Grace's favorite food is pizza.
2. Poppy's favorite sport is surfing.
3. Dylan's favorite animal is his horse.
4. Justin's favorite country is Australia.
5. Ling's favorite pastime is knitting.
6. Abdul's favorite color is purple.
7. Mira's favorite number is 10.
8. Jacob's favorite sweater is woolen.
9. Tori's favorite relative is her cousin.

42.6 🔊
1. Sam's **favorite band** is Big Bang.
2. Joe's favorite band is **Fun Sounds**.
3. Joni's **favorite restaurant** is Midnight Pizza.
4. Sam's favorite restaurant is **The Salad Bar**.
5. Joe's **favorite restaurant** is Burger Heaven.
6. Joni **loves the play** called Big Blue Sea.
7. Joe loves the movie called **Blue Soul**.

42.7
1. yoga
2. burgers
3. surfing
4. a restaurant

44

44.4 🔊
1. Paul cannot ride a bicycle.
2. Manuel cannot come to the party.
3. They can sleep in the tent tonight.
4. I cannot walk up the hill.
5. I can carry this box to the car.

44.5 🔊
1. Jo's pen doesn't work. She **can't** write her letter.
2. I understand the homework, so I **can** do it.
3. The museum is closed. We **can't** get in.
4. I have the car today, so I **can** drive you.
5. It's cold outside, so we **can't** have a picnic.
6. Tony needs to work late, so he **can't** come.
7. We **can't** play tennis. It's too dark.

44.6
1. Shirley can drive a car. Shirley can't drive a car.
2. Ben and Julie cannot carry boxes. Ben and Julie can't carry boxes.
3. Ilaria can spell English words. Ilaria cannot spell English words.
4. He can go to work. He can't go to work.

44.9 🔊
1. No, **he can't.**
2. Yes, **they can.**
3. No, **I can't.**
4. Yes, **I can.**
5. No, **we can't.**
6. Yes, **she can.**
7. No, **they can't.**

44.10 🔊
1. Can the dog jump over the wall?
2. Can Denise touch her toes?
3. Can I lift my son onto my shoulders?
4. Can Grandma see the TV?
5. Can I hit the tennis ball over the net?

44.11
1. True
2. False
3. True
4. True

44.12 🔊
1. Paul and Jerry don't like the ocean because they **cannot** swim.
2. I ride my bike to work because I **cannot** drive.
3. Jim cannot climb over the wall, but he **can** walk around it.
4. My mother **cannot** lift that bag because it's too heavy.
5. My sister Penny loves music and **can** dance to any song.

45

45.3 🔊
1 Mary can speak French **excellently**.
2 Roger can run very **quickly**.
3 The old man walks **slowly**.
4 He talks very **loudly**.
5 She won the race **easily**.

45.5
REGULAR
loudly, quickly, badly, easily
IRREGULAR
fast, well, hard, early

45.6 🔊
1 You speak English very **well**.
2 Damian cooks burgers **badly**.
3 I can get to your house **easily**.
4 Benjy always listens **carefully**.
5 My brother always works **hard**.
6 Sammy always plays his guitar **loudly**.

45.10 🔊
1 My horse is good at jumping.
2 I am bad at getting up early.
3 Mary is bad at writing German.
4 Jo and Bob are good at swimming.
5 Millie is bad at cleaning.

45.11 🔊
1 Conchita is good at playing basketball.
2 You can drive a van well.
3 Shania and Dave are good at surfing.
4 My father can't speak English well.
5 Manu is bad at writing stories.

45.12
1 Bad at
2 Bad at
3 Bad at
4 Good at

45.13 🔊
1. I am good at cooking.
2. I am bad at cooking.
3. I am good at playing soccer.
4. I am bad at playing soccer.
5. I am good at history.
6. I am bad at history.
7. He is good at cooking.
8. He is bad at cooking.
9. He is good at playing soccer.
10. He is bad at playing soccer.
11. He is good at history.
12. He is bad at history.

46

46.3 🔊
1 A tortoise walks very slowly.
2 A chicken flies quite badly.
3 Pigs eat very noisily.
4 Monkeys climb trees really well.

46.5
1 Really good
2 Quite good
3 Quite good
4 Really good

47

47.4
1 He wants to get a dog.
He would like to get a dog.
2 You want to work in Turkey.
You'd like to work in Turkey.
3 We would like to learn Chinese.
We'd like to learn Chinese.
4 They want to start a rock band.
They would like to start a rock band.

47.5 🔊
1 He'd like to act in a musical.
2 He wants to be in the Olympics.
3 He'd like to travel around Asia.
4 She'd like to sail a boat.
5 She wants to work with lions in Africa.

47.6 🔊
1. I'd like to climb this tree.
2. I'd like to climb that mountain.
3. I'd like to read a newspaper.
4. I'd like to read another book.
5. I want to climb this tree.
6. I want to climb that mountain.
7. I want to read a newspaper.
8. I want to read another book.
9. She wants to climb this tree.
10. She wants to climb that mountain.
11. She wants to read a newspaper.
12. She wants to read another book.

47.9
1 He would not like to play tennis.
He wouldn't like to play tennis.
2 She would not like to study science.
She doesn't want to study science.
3 They would not like to go to work.
They wouldn't like to go to work.
4 You wouldn't like to sing.
You don't want to sing.

5 We would not like to go diving.
We don't want to go diving.

47.11
1 No, she wouldn't.
2 Yes, he does.
3 Yes, he would.
4 No, she doesn't.
5 Yes, she would.

47.12 🔊
1 He doesn't want to climb that hill.
2 I wouldn't like to be a judge.
3 They don't want to go to work today.
4 She would like to play tennis tonight.
5 I want to climb that tree.

48

48.5 🔊
1 Jerry would really like to pass his driving test.
2 Ben and Sam would really like to take an IELTS test.
3 Helen would quite like to practice her English.
4 I'd quite like to play the piano tonight.

48.6 🔊
1. I'd really like to practice my spelling.
2. I'd really like to do a biology degree.
3. I'd really like to learn English.
4. I'd quite like to practice my spelling.
5. I'd quite like to do a biology degree.
6. I'd quite like to learn English.
7. Laila would really like to pass her history exam.
8. Laila would really like to do a biology degree.
9. Laila would really like to learn English.
10. Laila would quite like to pass her history exam.
11. Laila would quite like to do a biology degree.
12. Laila would quite like to learn English.

48.9 🔊
1 Emily has **a lovely home**.
2 Sue always takes her lunch to **the office**.
3 Can you see where **the church** is?
4 Jim went to **bed** hours ago.
5 Can you drive me into **town** later?
6 I live next to **the university**.
7 I leave **home** at 8am every weekday.

48.10
1 Tom
2 Frank
3 Sophie
4 Charlie
5 Sarah

Índice

Las entradas se indican por el número de la unidad. Las principales aparecen en **negrita**.

Agradecimientos

Los editores expresan su agradecimiento a:
Jo Kent, Trish Burrow y Emma Watkins por la redacción de textos adicionales; Thomas Booth, Helen Fanthorpe, Helen Leech, Carrie Lewis y Vicky Richards por su asistencia editorial; Stephen Bere, Sarah Hilder, Amy Child, Fiona Macdonald y Simon Murrell por sus tareas de diseño; Simon Mumford por los mapas y banderas de países; Peter Chrisp por la comprobacion de datos; Penny Hands, Amanda Learmonth y Carrie Lewis por la corrección de pruebas; Elizabeth Wise por el índice; Tatiana Boyko, Rory Farrell, Clare Joyce y Viola Wang por sus ilustraciones adicionales; Liz Hammond por la edición de los guiones de audio y la gestión de las grabaciones; Hannah Bowen y Scarlett O'Hara por compilar los guiones de audio; George Flamouridis por hacer las mezclas y el master de las grabaciones de audio; Heather Hughes, Tommy Callan, Tom Morse, Gillian Reid y Sonia Charbonnier por su apoyo técnico creativo; Vishal Bhatia, Kartik Gera, Sachin Gupta, Shipra Jain, Deepak Mittal, Nehal Verma, Roohi Rais, Jaileen Kaur, Anita Yadav, Manish Upreti, Nisha Shaw, Ankita Yadav y Priyanka Kharbanda por su asistencia técnica.

Todas las imágenes son propiedad de DK.
Para más información se puede visitar:
www.dkimages.com